MW00399563

Desktop
Devotions
for
Working
Mothers

DESKTOP
DEVOTIONS
for WORKING
MOTHERS

E L S A   H O U T Z

NAVPRESS

BRINGING TRUTH TO LIFE

NavPress Publishing Group

P.O. Box 35001, Colorado Springs, Colorado 80935

The Navigators is an international Christian organization. Jesus Christ gave His followers the Great Commission to go and make disciples (Matthew 28:19). The aim of The Navigators is to help fulfill that commission by multiplying laborers for Christ in every nation.

NavPress is the publishing ministry of The Navigators. NavPress publications are tools to help Christians grow. Although publications alone cannot make disciples or change lives, they can help believers learn biblical discipleship, and apply what they learn to their lives and ministries.

Library of Congress Catalog Card Number:
92-40356
ISBN 08910-97198

The anecdotal illustrations in this book are composites of real situations, and any resemblance to people living or dead is coincidental.

Unless otherwise identified, all Scripture quotations in this publication are taken from the *HOLY BIBLE: NEW INTER-NATIONAL VERSION®* (NIV®). Copyright © 1973, 1978, 1984 by International Bible Society. Used by permission of Zondervan Publishing House. All rights reserved. Another version used is the *King James Version* (KJV).

Houtz, Elsa, 1950-
    Desktop devotions for working mothers / Elsa Houtz.
        p.   cm.
    ISBN 0-89109-719-8 :
    1. Working mothers—Prayer-books and devotions—English. 2. Spirituality—Christianity.   I. Title.
BV4529.H68   1993
242'.8431—dc20   92-40356
                                                             CIP

Printed in the United States of America

FOR A FREE CATALOG OF
NAVPRESS BOOKS & BIBLE STUDIES,
CALL 1-800-366-7788 (USA)
or 1-416-499-4615 (CANADA)

CONTENTS

*To the glory of God
and to my son, Matt, with love*

PART ONE

WORKING
+
MOTHER
=
HELP!

I'M COMING APART AT THE SEAMS

*When she heard about Jesus, she came up
behind him in the crowd and touched
his cloak, because she thought, "If I just
touch his clothes, I will be healed." . . .
He said to her,
"Daughter, your faith has healed you."*
Mark 5:27-28,34

TODAY'S TO-DO LIST

❧ Reach out to experience Christ's healing touch when life feels fragmented and torn

L ittle Jenny is playing with a teddy bear. Her brother Matthew, seeing it, decides now would be an excellent time for *him* to play with the teddy bear. He grabs one of its legs, while Jenny staunchly clings to one of its arms. They try to wrestle it away from each other. Suddenly there's a ripping sound and a flurry of flying stuffing. The children both begin to cry, and there's the poor teddy bear, lying on the floor with a split seam, looking sad indeed.

Do you ever feel like that bear, pulled apart and torn by conflicting demands of the many roles and responsibilities you're called on to fulfill?

You promised your boss you'd work late Thursday night. On Wednesday your husband calls you at work. He excitedly tells you he has been selected to receive an award from his civic club the next night and he really wants you to be at the awards dinner with him. Ri-i-i-ip. You feel torn.

You've just finished a big project at work. Now you can finally do some catching up. The next morning, your toddler wakes up with the chicken pox. Ri-i-i-i-ip.

Your best friend is expecting a baby, and her sister is having a baby shower. You really want to go, but it's the only night all week your whole family could be home together. Ri-i-i-ip.

One great difficulty faced by mothers who work outside the home is the tug of conflicting roles and responsibilities—commitments to employers, children, spouses, parents, friends, church, community, even self. This sense of being pulled apart stems not only from trying to juggle conflicting time commitments, but also from roles that make competing demands: parent versus employee, spouse versus parent, community volunteer versus church member versus parent versus spouse, and so on. It's hard to maintain a sense of wholeness in the midst of so much internal conflict.

I believe the story in Mark 5:25-34 of the woman who came to Jesus for healing has rich promises for those of us who feel torn and fragmented by the demands of everyday life. Foremost is the promise of healing—healing for our sense of inner conflict, healing for the loss of self that results as we race schizophrenically from one role to another.

Jesus has always been able to see clearly what people need from Him. Even when this sick woman came up behind Him, unseen, He recognized her need for healing. We can easily imagine that He knew immediately of her loneliness and isolation resulting from years of being shunned as "unclean" because of her illness. Surely He sensed the frustration and hopelessness she felt after spending everything she had on cures and treatments, with no success. Her spirit, as well as her body, cried out to be healed.

Think for a moment of what it would have been like to be in that woman's place. Think of how she must have felt when Jesus spoke to her: "Daughter, your faith has healed you. Go in peace and be freed from your suffering" (Mark 5:34). In that moment she received from Jesus not only healing, but freedom from suffering—emotional, spiritual, physical—as well. After giving up all hope, after resigning herself to a life of rejection and despair, she found herself restored to health. What a moment!

Most modern translations of the Bible quote Jesus as saying, "Your faith has healed you." I especially like the wording of the *King James Version*: "Daughter, thy faith hath made thee whole; go in peace, and be whole of thy plague" (Mark 5:34, KJV). Isn't wholeness what we really want in our crazy lives of fulfilling this role and that role? We want to feel like whole women, complete, real and worthwhile, apart from the many identities we assume in order to meet others' expectations. We want to be sewn back together, not fragmented and torn.

Jesus promises us that healing, that wholeness. Just as He knew the needs of the sick woman before He even saw her, He knows that we need a sense of our own personhood—our importance and worth apart from the tasks we do and the roles we fill. We can't obtain that sense of wholeness by working harder or doing more or reading pop psychology or becoming fitness fanatics. We receive it only when we reach out, believing, to receive Christ's love and power.

The Greek word for "healed," which is used in Mark's gospel, also means "saved." The healing and wholeness Jesus Christ promises is linked to our salvation through Him. It is our *faith* that saves us—saves us from eternal death and from a fragmented, guilt-ridden, unsatisfying life.

When we feel pulled apart, worn out by conflicting responsibilities, we can find joy instead by hearing Jesus' comforting words: "Daughter, thy faith hath made thee whole."

❦PRAYER❧

*Dear God, thank You for the story of this
long-ago woman whose simple faith
has so much to teach me.
I know that often I look for my identity
and importance in the things I do
and the roles I fulfill. Teach me
to reach out
for Christ's loving touch instead.*
AMEN.

TWO

I'M DEFINITELY INTERESTED

*Each of you should look
not only to his own interests,
but also to the interests of others.*

Philippians 2:4

⊸ Monitor the balance in my life
between my own needs and the
needs of those around me

Have you noticed that most playgrounds built during the past fifteen
years or so don't have teeter-totters?
The people who design playgrounds decided
some years ago that teeter-totters were the
cause of so many accidents and injuries that
playgrounds were safer without them.

That's not too hard to understand. If you,
like me, grew up with teeter-totters, you can
identify with the following incident.

During recess, Janie and her best friend,
Debbie, are happily teeter-tottering, pushing
off with their feet and riding gently up and
down. Along comes the class bully, Chuckie.
He sits down behind Janie on the teeter-totter
seat, so that the extra weight leaves Debbie
stranded high up off the ground. Then, he

pushes Janie off her seat and quickly jumps off, causing Debbie's end of the teeter-totter to crash to the ground—with her on it. She tumbles off and begins to cry. Janie starts to hit Chuckie. Someone runs to tell the teacher. . . . It's easy to see why teeter-totters aren't so common anymore.

The key to happy teeter-tottering, of course, is balance. When Chuckie came along and destroyed the balance, two things happened: (1) When Chuckie put too much weight on Janie's end, Debbie was stranded up off the ground, helpless to do anything short of jumping off; (2) when Chuckie removed all the weight from Janie's side, Debbie crashed to the ground and got hurt.

Balance is essential in our everyday lives, too—balance between job and home, between work and leisure, between what Paul calls our own interests and the interests of others. I believe the balance of "interests" is the hardest for working mothers to achieve and maintain.

The consequences of losing this balance are much the same as they are on the teeter-totter: We either flail around ineffectively, stranded in feelings of helplessness, guilt, and failure: or we crash from over-commitment and burnout that leave us feeling bruised and battered.

Christ gave us the key to maintaining a balance of interests in His most basic instruction about loving our neighbors—"Love your neighbor as yourself." In that simple command, He taught us something about the importance that He wants us to assign to ourselves: not an egocentric, me-first importance, but a fundamental respect for ourselves as His creations and His agents on earth. If we do not love and value ourselves, we have no basis on which to love and value others. In other words, *our loving and caring for others needs to be modeled on a healthy love and concern for ourselves.* We need to learn to balance others' needs—their "interests"—and our own.

The apostle Paul explained this connection clearly in Romans 13:9—"The commandments, 'Do not commit adultery,' 'Do not murder,' 'Do not steal,' 'Do not covet,' and whatever other commandment there may be, are summed up in this one rule: 'Love your neighbor as yourself.'" We seek to avoid hurting others just as we seek to avoid hurting ourselves.

As babies, we learned to look out for ourselves by making sure we got enough to eat, enough rest, and enough dry diapers. We didn't worry at all about anyone else's needs; just getting our own needs met was a full-time job.

As we grew, we learned the importance of concern for others. And then, for many of us, the pendulum began to swing too far. Caught in the whirlwind of job, home, and family, we forgot how to take care of ourselves. We began investing so much time and energy in meeting the needs of employers, children, spouses, friends, extended family, church, and community that we began to neglect our own needs.

Unlike babies, now we, as working mothers, often don't eat properly and don't get enough rest. Although we no longer have to worry about being stuck with wet diapers (our own, anyway), we do sometimes neglect our own comfort and well-being. We don't take time for exercise or relaxation or friendship or entertainment. When we do make time for ourselves, we feel guilty because there are so many other things we think we should be doing. Our lives are out of balance.

I believe that God not only gives us permission to take time for ourselves and to do things for our own enjoyment and enrichment, but that He instructs us to do so. How can we reach out to others in compassion and service if we let ourselves become empty inside, or weakened and defeated by self-neglect? By attending to our own physical, emotional, social, and spiritual needs, we better equip ourselves to obey Jesus' command to "look to the interests of others."

Certainly He directs us to nurture, support, encourage, and care for those around us, but He also wants us to sustain ourselves so that we may serve Him to the greatest extent.

❧PRAYER❧

*God, I thank You that You care about me
even when I don't care enough about myself.
Instruct me in finding the balance
between my own needs and the needs
of those around me.
I love them all so much—
my family, friends, church,
the needy in my community.
Teach me also to love myself in a way
that best equips me to serve as You
would want me to serve.*
AMEN.

THREE

WHAT GOES AROUND COMES AROUND

A generous man will prosper; he who refreshes others will himself be refreshed.

Proverbs 11:25

"If you believe, you will receive whatever you ask for in prayer."

Matthew 21:22

TODAY'S TO-DO LIST
⌖ Practice both gracious giving
and gracious receiving

Therese is a woman I have known since I dated her son in high school (yes, ancient history!). He and I went our separate ways after our teenage romance, but Therese and I stayed friends for many years. One year, when I was home from college for the Christmas holiday, I met her for lunch at a little downtown restaurant.

After we had finished our lunch and were getting ready to leave, she said, "I have something to give you. I didn't gift-wrap it because then you'd think it was a Christmas present and you'd feel like you had to give me a gift in return. I just wanted to give you something, so here it is."

She put a paper sack on the table. Inside, nestled in a jumble of tissue paper, was a

Christmas tree ornament—a red-feathered bird perched on a nest made of shredded gold paper. Inside the nest were tiny, tiny Christmas-tree balls, like gleaming miniature bird eggs.

I still have that ornament. Every year, when I put it on my tree, I remember what Therese taught me about both giving and receiving. Her gift to me was simply a gesture of generosity and friendship, not prompted by holiday gift-giving protocols. She wanted me to receive her gift in the same spirit in which she gave it, and not feel guilty because I wasn't able to respond in kind.

How do you think Therese would have felt if I had said, "Gee, Therese, this is really nice, but I can't accept it because I don't have a gift for you"? Yet often we find it hard to accept the gifts of others when we can't reciprocate or don't feel that we are staying "even." Somewhere along the line we acquire a score-keeping mentality, and we're reluctant to let others outscore us in giving.

Previously we've talked about the importance of balancing our needs and the needs of others in order to live effectively for Christ. Another important balance, I believe, is between giving and receiving.

We know that the Bible says "it is more blessed to give than to receive" (Acts 20:35), and also contains numerous instructions about giving generously and cheerfully to others. We often overlook, though, the Bible's instruction in *receiving*. We feel that, as Christians, we must always be giving, never receiving or accepting anything from others.

This give-only philosophy is out of keeping with our relationship with God. His nature is one that gives constantly, generously, and unconditionally, and we simply receive. Nothing we can give back to Him could begin to repay the gift of Christ's sacrifice on the cross, or the gift of our very lives. Even when we give our total commitment to serving and obeying Him, our gift is nothing compared to His gifts to us. "He is not served by human hands, as if he needed anything, because he himself gives all men life and breath and everything else" (Acts 17:25).

Jesus described clearly how we are to receive from God: "I tell you the truth, anyone who will not receive the kingdom of God like a little child will never enter it" (Luke 18:17). Think about a child receiving a Christmas present or a trinket from a relative. Do children worry about how they'll repay that person? Do they feel obligated or compelled to find something to give in return? No. They simply receive, accept, and enjoy.

Some people find it harder to receive than others. Have you ever offered to help a coworker with her workload, only to hear, "No, that's okay, I'll get it done somehow"? Have you repeatedly offered to help a friend with carpooling or babysitting and been told, "No, I can do it"? Or are you someone who finds it difficult to receive? If someone unexpectedly gives you a birthday gift or Christmas present, do you feel required to run out and buy one to give in exchange?

I'm not sure why we sometimes find it hard to receive the kindness of others. Maybe it makes us feel inadequate to think we need someone else's help or generosity. Maybe we're so locked into our score-keeping mindset that we can't stand to "owe" anyone, even when they don't expect us to repay them. Maybe we're so accustomed to having to do things ourselves that we've forgotten how to let others help us. Maybe we feel noble and spiritually correct only when we give and not when we receive.

Whatever the reason, I think we hurt ourselves when we refuse to receive the gifts others offer us. If we cannot receive from others, we are in danger of forgetting how to receive from God . . . like a little child. Scripture tells us there is joy in giving. When we cannot let others give to us, we cheat them of that joy and we cheat ourselves of the joy of receiving their kindness.

❦PRAYER❦

*Father God, You give us so much.
Show me the balance between giving
and receiving. I want to always give
wholeheartedly, selflessly, and cheerfully.
Help me learn to receive from others—
and from You—in the same spirit.*
AMEN.

FOUR

THE VACUUM FACTOR

Jesus answered, "It says:
'Do not put the Lord your God to the test.'"
Luke 4:12

Vacuuming is not my favorite household chore. For one thing, it makes my back hurt. I see commercials for new, lightweight vacuum cleaners that are supposed to make vacuuming a breeze, but mine isn't one of those. I'm sure it weighs as much as I do. It blows out at least as much dust and dirt as it sweeps up, and when it sucks up paper clips or thumbtacks, it sounds like a spoon is caught in the garbage disposal.

That's why I was pretty surprised when my friend Cathy said she had begun to see vacuuming as a spiritual lesson.

What?

Cathy is a college student who spent last summer working as a housekeeper at a resort. Her main job was to clean and vacuum the guests' cabins, which had wall-to-wall carpeting. Since vacuuming doesn't demand a lot of thought, she found herself reflecting on other things as she ran the vacuum cleaner.

"When I vacuum a cabin," she told me, "I plug in the vacuum cleaner in one room, vacuum that room, and then leave the cord plugged in there and go on to another room. Eventually the cord gets stretched too far. It pops out of the socket, and the vacuum cleaner goes off when I'm right in the middle of vacuuming that next room. And I have to stop and plug it in somewhere closer.

"If I had bothered to moved the plug into the next room in the first place, that wouldn't happen—but out of pure laziness, I try to avoid the tiny, little extra bit of work involved in moving it to another outlet. And then the power goes off, and I have to re-plug it in anyway.

"I realized one day that I do much the same thing in my spiritual life. I see how far away from God I can get, how far I can push His grace, before I 'lose power' and start to feel out of touch with Him. I move farther and farther away from the Source of power in my life, and then I have to go through a period of spiritual rebuilding and reconnecting with Him.

"It's so foolish of me to do that. Why

don't I stay close to Him all the time and stay 'plugged in,' instead of trying to test both His and my limits? I know it's a case of spiritual laziness, just like it's physical laziness that makes me try to stretch the vacuum cord beyond its limits."

Do you find that, like Cathy, you sometimes get too far away from the Source of power in your life—so far, in fact, that you eventually feel as though God's power has been cut off? Do you "test" God's love by moving farther and farther away until you begin to feel isolated or estranged from Him?

We know that God never moves away from us; His love is constant. The Source of power never changes. We're the ones who move. We wander, we stray, we see how far we can disobey and disregard Him before we start to feel the painful consequences, within us and outside us in circumstances, events, and relationships.

We make little day-to-day decisions, say things, do things, that we know aren't pleasing to Him, but we also find ways to rationalize them. Then we start to make even bigger choices that move us farther away from His path. And then, because we don't want to be uncomfortable with those choices, we start to avoid thinking about His commands and His instructions to us—and about Him altogether—because that makes us squirm.

Eventually, something happens—a family crisis, an unexpected problem, a financial disaster, a broken relationship—that makes demands on our spiritual strength. We suddenly wonder why we feel so unable to cope, so spiritually powerless. We have let ourselves become "unplugged" by failing to maintain a close connection with God.

Believe it or not, every time I haul out my vacuum cleaner now, I use it as an opportunity to check my spiritual "distance." Have I been lazy, wandering as far as I can from God's desires, while still wanting to enjoy the blessings of His love and grace? Or have I worked to stay close to the Source of power, to stay in touch with Him through prayer, reflection, and the study of His Word every day?

I still don't like vacuuming. But now, as I push that heavy, old vacuum cleaner around my house, moving the plug from room to room, I think about the power God offers us, the power that comes from His infinite greatness, His limitless love, and His unfailing wisdom. All of it is ours for the asking. What an energizer.

When I've finished vacuuming my house, my back still hurts—but there's a smile on my face.

Thanks, Cathy.

❧PRAYER❧

Dear Lord, help me to stay close to You.
Give me the discipline
to guard my own path, to know when
spiritual laziness causes me
to wander away from You,
the Source of power in my life.
Thank You for Your constancy
and faithfulness.
AMEN.

FIVE

GETTING TO THE HEART OF THINGS

I will praise you, O Lord my God,
with all my heart;
I will glorify your name forever.

Psalm 86:12

"**M**y heart isn't in this."

"I didn't have the heart to tell her about it."

"It was a pretty halfhearted effort, if you ask me."

"Please accept my heartfelt sympathy."

Our language is full of expressions pertaining to the heart. Although we know, scientifically, that the heart is a muscle that pumps blood throughout the body, we still talk about it as the home of our emotions, our innermost feelings, and our deepest desires.

The Bible reflects this symbolic importance of the heart in literally hundreds of verses. It instructs us repeatedly to "take to heart" God's commands (Deuteronomy 4:39) and to "love the Lord your God with all your heart" (Matthew 22:37).

We experience "heart trouble" when we recognize that something is wrong at the very core of our being; something is preventing us from experiencing the deep-down peace and joy that God promises. Maybe a lingering resentment gnaws at our peace of mind, a persistent fear blocks us from venturing into new things, or perhaps a chronic insecurity simply defeats us day after day.

Heart trouble takes many forms. The Bible offers the diagnosis—and the treatment—for several common ailments of the heart.

Faintheartedness is a weariness of the spirit. When we are fainthearted, we feel as though we haven't the strength or the courage or the energy to follow through on our commitments or to deal with our problems. We don't feel strong enough to stand apart from the crowd or to fight temptation, hopelessness, or despair. Giving up starts to seem like our best option.

God stands ready to encourage us when we feel fainthearted. When we turn to Him and ask for His sustaining grace, He offers us the strength and the courage to deal with whatever life brings. The psalmist David, under attack from powerful enemies, asked God to restore him when he felt himself growing fainthearted: "From the ends of the earth I call to you, I call as my heart grows faint; lead me to the rock that is higher than I. For you have been my refuge, a strong tower against the foe" (Psalm 61:2-3).

Hardheartedness afflicts us when we become unresponsive to God's guidance and direction in our lives. We disregard the needs of those around us and feel no responsibility to carry out God's work in the world. We make choices and take action based on worldly or selfish considerations, instead of on His commands.

Hardheartedness can develop in us gradually, like the slow buildup of a callus. Our ability to recognize God's voice becomes diminished bit by bit, until we find ourselves out of touch with Him.

The Bible warns us against letting this happen: "But encourage one another daily . . . so that none of you may be hardened by sin's deceitfulness. . . . 'Today, if you hear his voice, do not harden your hearts'" (Hebrews 3:13,15). Maintaining openness to God's work in our lives and acting in obedience to His commands is the best preventive medicine against hardheartedness.

Halfheartedness is an ailment caused by less-than-full commitment to Christ. We may say that we want Him to reign as Lord in our lives, but only a part of us is truly committed—another part still wants to live by the world's standards.

The halfhearted person doubts God's ability to meet her needs and wants to rely on the world instead. The apostle James describes the person in this condition as "a double-minded man, unstable in all he does" (James 1:8). The halfhearted person is destined to live a life of uncertainty and disappointment, never reaping the full abundance of God's blessings.

In contrast, the Bible directs us to live not halfheartedly but wholeheartedly for the Lord, to love Him with all our hearts, souls, minds, and strength. As Deuteronomy states, "You will find him if you look for him with all your heart and with all your soul" (4:29).

Brokenheartedness is a condition of such intense inner pain that we truly feel as if a part of us has been physically broken. The loss of a loved one, a life-shattering disappointment, helplessness in the face of another person's suffering—these are some things that leave us feeling brokenhearted.

Only God's healing touch can repair a broken heart. Only the sure knowledge of His infinite power can reassure us that we will be whole again, even when our lives are filled with pain. As Jesus said, "I have told you these things, so that in me you may have peace. In this world you will have trouble. But take heart! I have overcome the world" (John 16:33).

There is no ailment of the human heart that God cannot cure.

❧PRAYER❧

God, I know that You see into my heart,
and I cannot hide from You.
I desire to live wholeheartedly for You,
with courage and commitment,
turning to receive Your healing touch
when my heart is in pain.
AMEN.

SIX

A
HEARTY
WELCOME

"Blessed are the pure in heart,
for they will see God."

Matthew 5:8

TODAY'S TO-DO LIST

🖎 Further examine the spiritual
   health of my own heart

W hen I worked as the editor of a
national church magazine, one of my
duties was to review the letters from
our denomination's missionaries and prepare
them for publication. I always looked forward
to reading news from the mission field. At
times it was like delving into an adventure
novel!

One letter was particularly memorable. It
was from a missionary wife in a remote part of
Africa. She wrote of the jungle climate, so
relentlessly hot and damp, and the daily challenges of living in primitive conditions without
even the most basic conveniences. Her
description of the origins of local foods and
the constant battle against disease-bearing par-
asites made my stomach cringe. And yet she

wrote of all these things with a joyful spirit, communicating a real sense of privilege to be serving God in that remote corner of His world. In her I saw a person who truly had a heart for the work she was doing.

Previously we looked at some of the ailments that can plague the human heart. But what makes a healthy heart? What does it mean to truly "have a heart for God" and for His work? When God looks into the heart of a Christian woman, what does He desire to see?

I believe Scripture suggests several qualities of the healthy heart for us to cultivate. Let's look at each one.

A healthy heart is a *willing* heart. When God commanded Moses to build His tabernacle and to provide its furnishings, Moses assembled all the artisans and skilled workers he would need to carry out the task. Exodus gives the account: "All who were willing, men and women alike, came. . . . Every skilled woman spun with her hands and brought what she had spun. . . . And all the women who were willing and had the skill spun the goat hair" (35:22,25-26,29).

Ability and skill were not enough to accomplish what God had commanded for the tabernacle, just as they are not enough to accomplish His work in our world today. God needs women with willing hearts who will put their gifts, talents, and resources to work for Him, not for their own gain.

God looks for a *sincere* heart. Deceit and insincerity have no place in the lives of Christian women. We cannot fool God, nor can we fool those around us for long. Jesus told us, "The good man brings good things out of the good stored up in his heart, and the evil man brings evil things out of the evil stored up in his heart. For out of the overflow of his heart his mouth speaks" (Luke 6:45). If we are to witness for Christ effectively, we must represent Him to others with sincerity and truth.

A healthy heart is *compassionate*. In the midst of our busy lives, as we become harried by the demands of job and family, it's easy to let compassion slip out of our hearts. The pressure of too little time and too many tasks, the fatigue that comes from pushing ourselves to the limit, the stress of juggling so many roles—all of these things can erode our compassion. Sometimes it takes all the energy we have simply to push ourselves through another day.

The woman described in Proverbs 31 is an inspiring model of a busy woman who still manages to be compassionate. While juggling a family, a busy household, and a demanding business, she still "opens her arms to the poor and extends her hands to the needy" (verse 20). Compassion can easily be squeezed out of our hearts unless we cultivate and nurture it by acts of kindness—a word of encouragement to a despairing friend, a gift to the needy, an act of volunteer service to someone who is suffering.

A healthy heart is *joyful*. You don't have to look very far in our world to find cause for sadness. No individual life is without private sorrows. A byproduct of compassion is the ability to feel others' pain. Yet God still calls us to joy, a joy that transcends outward events, a joy anchored in the hope of what eternity with God offers.

Unlike happiness, which depends on circumstances, true joy stems from the assurance that we have a place with God forever. The psalmist recognized this hope: "You have made known to me the path of life; you will fill me with joy in your presence, with eternal pleasures at your right hand" (Psalm 16:11); "Your statutes are my heritage forever; they are the joy of my heart" (Psalm 119:111).

God looks for a *courageous* heart. If there were ever a time when Christian women needed courage, it is now. Ungodly forces snatch at our children before our very eyes—through the media, in our schools, on the streets of our own neighborhoods. Pressures for self-indulgence and sexual license threaten our marriages and the very foundations of our homes. The Christian values that were once adopted by the majority are now viewed as reactionary and out of step.

Those who put their faith in God are severely outnumbered. More than ever, we need hearts full of courage. We must continue to fight for our loved ones, for our faith, for our identity as women of God.

Let's take to heart God's encouraging words to Joshua: "Have I not commanded you? Be strong and courageous. Do not be terrified; do not be discouraged, for the LORD your God will be with you wherever you go" (Joshua 1:9).

❧PRAYER❧

Dear Lord God,
search my heart and show me where I
am lacking. Fill my heart with willingness,
sincerity, compassion, joy, and courage.
I want to live wholeheartedly for You.
AMEN.

SEVEN

SIGN ON THE DOTTED LINE

*In the same way, after the supper
[Jesus] took the cup, saying,
"This cup is the new covenant in my
blood, which is poured out for you."*

Luke 22:20

TODAY'S TO-DO LIST

- Review the "covenants" of my life
- Reaffirm the promises I made in those covenants

MEMORANDUM

To: Mr. Charles Grady, Supervisor,
        Research Department
From: Gwen Thompson, Research Assistant
Re: Job Description

As you know, part of my job description entails compiling the data from our field offices into monthly reports. However, after holding this job for six months, I have determined that I don't especially like preparing the reports. It's very time-consuming, and well, let's face it, it's boring. Therefore, I have decided not to do it anymore. Please assign the task to someone else. Thank you.

MEMORANDUM

To: My kids—Kim and Lindsay
From: Gwen (Mom)
Re: Parenting

You kids are great, but you're really a lot of work. Coping with all your emotional ups and downs (especially this teenage stuff, Lindsay!), helping you with school, driving you all over town, listening to your problems when I'm tired and have so much else on my mind. . . . Well, it's just too much, so I've decided to take early retirement. So, from here on out, you kids will need to raise yourselves. Your dad will be glad to help, I'm sure.

    You're very smart kids. I know you'll do a great job.

MEMORANDUM

To: My husband, Gene
From: Gwen
Re: Marriage

During the past year or so, I've begun to wonder if we're really right for each other. I mean, where's the magic that we had when we were first married? And my life is so demanding—taking care of the house and the kids, holding down a job, being a wife. I can't help thinking my life would be a little more, you know, *excit-*

ing if I weren't married to you. Thanks for understanding, and have a great life.

❧

MEMORANDUM

To: Pastor Don Clark,
        First Christian Church
From: Gwen Thompson
Re: Being a Christian

When I first heard you preach about being a Christian, it sounded great—being loved, having eternal life, receiving forgiveness, what a deal! But I have to tell you, it's turned out to be a lot harder than I thought—obeying all those commandments, loving others, being kind, etc., etc.

I was wondering if maybe there was some less difficult approach to being a Christian—maybe like being an honorary one or something, where I could still go to church but not really have to do all those other things. Do you think that could be arranged?

❧

Gwen wants to renegotiate the contracts in her life—in her job, her parenting role, her marriage, her spiritual life. Things aren't turning out like she thought they would.

Like Gwen, all of us enter into numerous covenants, or agreements, in our lives. We promise that we will do certain things, fulfill certain commitments. Because we are human, though, at times we find ourselves wishing that we could change the terms of those covenants.

Sometimes it's because we lack the perseverance to ride out the difficulties in a job or a relationship. Sometimes we don't have the vision to see that the problems are temporary or to find a positive way to deal with them. Sometimes we can't summon enough hope or haven't experienced enough faith to believe that we can surmount the obstacles before us. Sometimes we're unwilling to make the sacrifices that our commitments require. Often it's simply hard.

Our covenant with God through Christ gives meaning and possibility to all the other commitments in our lives. His Spirit in us can give us the ability to persevere, to believe, to hope, to stand firm, to joyfully fulfill the terms of our other covenants.

Without being firmly established in our reliance on God, we're forced to rely on human strength and wisdom. The psalmist says that a righteous person "keeps his oath even when it hurts" (Psalm 15:4). Our human nature doesn't give that kind of strength and endurance, but the Holy Spirit does.

Think about the commitments in your life—parenthood, work, marriage, church, community service, and others. Are there ways you can rely more on God's power and less on yourself to fully honor those promises?

❧PRAYER❧

Father God, I thank You
for Your faithfulness to me, even
at those times when I fail terribly in my
commitments to You and others.
Help me to honor all the important
covenants in my life.
AMEN.

EIGHT

TIME FOR A NEW TURKEY

*"I will give you a new heart and put a
new spirit in you; I will remove from you
your heart of stone and give you a heart
of flesh. And I will put my Spirit in you
and move you to follow my decrees
and be careful to keep my laws."*

Ezekiel 36:26-27

TODAY'S TO-DO LIST

- Examine my heart to see where I'm harboring old, negative, destructive feelings
- With God's help, dispose of them

Several years ago, I was in a play that included a big Thanksgiving dinner scene—complete with a real turkey, roasted to a golden brown. After every performance, the props coordinator would take the turkey home and put it in her freezer, then thaw it out the next day for that night's performance.

As the play was performed night after night for more than a week, that poor turkey began to show signs of hardship from being frozen and thawed over and over again. It looked perfect to the audience, but to those of us close to it on the stage, it was highly unappetizing.

One night, after the play had been performed several times, I noticed Bill, the leading man of the show, looking pensively at the stage set for the Thanksgiving dinner scene. He was a very talented actor (who later appeared in several TV series), and I always liked to hear his ideas.

"You look so deep in thought," I said to him. "What's on your mind?"

"I think," he said with great deliberation, "that it's time for a new turkey."

🍂

Over the years I've discovered that, in many areas of my life, the time eventually comes for a new turkey: that is, a new outlook or a fresh set of attitudes, beliefs, or feelings about a specific person or circumstance.

For example, I'd have a bad experience in working with a particular person at the office, and then I'd keep the negative memory of that experience stored up so that my feelings toward that person never changed. Or I'd decide that I wasn't good at a certain role or task, and let the burden of that decision keep me from trying to grow and improve. Or I'd let myself become defeated because a certain area of my spiritual life didn't seem to be working, and I'd carry around that sense of defeat instead of finding the victory Christ promised.

How about you? Are there turkeys in your life that need to be thrown out and replaced with something better? Are you harboring negative, destructive feelings or attitudes in a relationship? In your perception of yourself? In your approach to some aspect of your job or your home responsibilities? In some area of your spiritual life where you've given up on trying to follow Christ's example? Most of us have old turkeys stowed away somewhere.

These old turkeys aren't always easy to spot. For one thing, we get used to them. Those of us who were in the play saw that turkey night after night, and we grew so used to it that none of us paid any attention to how it looked. When we fall into the habit of feeling a certain way about a person or situation, after a while we don't pay any attention to those feelings—they eventually become a part of us.

Our turkey in the play looked fine to the audience, too, just as we can keep people around us from seeing the "turkeys" we're harboring inside. We can outwardly portray a friendly or positive attitude while inwardly we're seething with unforgiveness, bitterness, or resentment. We're all pretty adept at keeping our "audience" from seeing what we don't want them to see.

In the play, the deterioration of our lovely golden-brown turkey into a discolored, wrinkled leftover was so gradual that no one really noticed until it was beyond salvaging. The un-Christlike attitudes we harbor inside can cause the same kind of gradual erosion of our spirits. This change can be so gradual that we may not even notice its effect, until one day we wake up and see that we've done something we bitterly regret or we've become someone we don't want to be.

How do we unload these old turkeys once we spot them? I think we can do it the same way the props coordinator for our play disposed of the decaying turkey: Put it in a garbage bag and throw it in the trash. Once we spot a long-standing, destructive attitude or an old, stale grievance, we can mentally bundle it up and toss it away, praising God for allowing us to be free of it as we cling to His promise of a new heart and a new spirit. Surely a God who created the universe and all that's in it stands ready to help us with the simple task of discarding old poultry.

❧PRAYER❧

God, it's so easy for me to store old hurts, petty resentment, and negative experiences in my heart. Please give me the strength to discard those useless, destructive feelings and seek the new spirit You promise.
AMEN.

NINE

JOINING THE JET SET

Those who know your name will trust in you, for you, LORD, have never forsaken those who seek you.

Psalm 9:10

TODAY'S TO-DO LIST

❧ Look for ways to practice putting my trust in God

Jan is the vice-president of an international computer company. For her, boarding a jet and flying from coast to coast, or from country to country, is as routine as driving to work is for you and me.

Jan uses her time on these plane trips to catch up on paperwork, to read, or just to relax and take a nap. She doesn't spend her time on the plane worrying about whether it will crash or be struck by lightning or catch fire.

Why doesn't she worry about these things?

Two reasons: First, because her experience has led her to have confidence in air travel. Even with the numerous trips she's taken, she's never found herself in danger or in fear for her safety. Even though she knows the hazards that exist, that knowledge is outweighed by the many safe trips she's had.

The second reason Jan doesn't worry is that, whether she's aware of it or not, she has placed her trust in the people connected with the airline—from the engineer who designed the aircraft to the technicians who service it and the crew members who fly it. The fact that she's never seen these people doesn't diminish her confidence in them.

In other words, when Jan boards that airplane, she's basically committing her well-being to a group of strangers. She doesn't know if the pilot is agitated because he had a fight with his wife that morning or was up all night with the flu. She doesn't know if the mechanic who was supposed to do the last-minute check on the plane was paying attention to what he was doing or if he was distracted with worry about a family crisis. She doesn't really know anything about any of these people, and yet she trusts them with her safety.

Each of us expresses this same kind of trust in other people every day. We trust other drivers on the road not to kill us—or we'd never venture out in our cars. We trust school teachers, administrators, babysitters, and day-care workers to supervise and educate our children. We trust doctors and nurses to make sound judgments about our physical health. We trust construction workers to build buildings that won't collapse when we're inside them.

Most of the time, we trust these people without even thinking about it. We simply could not function in day-to-day life without a willingness to trust others, even those we may not know at all.

Yet, ironically, it's sometimes very hard for us to trust God in the same way. NonChristians often say that they don't believe in God because they can't see Him, yet they don't hesitate to put their faith in an airline technician they've never seen. Even Christians who believe unswervingly that God exists may have a difficult time truly trusting Him to care for them and their loved ones in the way He promises to do.

Jan trusts the airline industry because her experience has taught her that air travel is, with rare exceptions, safe. What does our experience of God teach us about Him? When we turn to Him with our needs, He answers us. When we ask Him for strength or wisdom, He gives it. When we commit our burdens to Him, we feel the lightness of being free from them. He keeps His promises. Our experience alone should teach us that He can be trusted. Even if we haven't yet experienced

His grace in our lives, we can see evidence of His goodness in the lives of other believers.

God's Word also expresses His promise that we can trust Him. When was the last time you heard an airline pilot come on the loud-speaker and say, "I absolutely, unequivocally promise I will fly you safely to your destination. Trust me"? A human being, no matter how well-equipped and well-trained, can't make that promise, because some things are outside of his control. But God can and does make an unqualified, no-holds-barred promise to care for us, and He is great enough to fulfill His promise. We may not understand all that goes on in this world, and things may happen to us that we wouldn't wish for, but God never defaults on His promise to care for us when we turn to Him.

Are there areas of your life where you find it especially hard to trust God? Is it hard to commit to God's care a child who's away at college or struggling with teenage temptations? Is it hard to believe that He truly can help you resolve a difficult work situation? Does it seem impossible that a marital conflict can ever be resolved or that you can survive the loss of a loved one? Are you ready to give up on an unbelieving spouse or a hateful coworker?

People like to say that only two things in

life are certain: death and taxes. As Christians, we know that isn't true. Something else is certain: God's faithfulness to us. "Cast your cares on the LORD and he will sustain you; he will never let the righteous fall," the psalmist tells us (Psalm 55:22). Now that's a promise we can truly trust.

❧PRAYER❧

My faithful, loving Father,
teach me to trust You more.
Wean me away from my need
for self-sufficiency and my insistence
on bearing my burdens alone.
Keep in my heart the sure knowledge
that You will sustain me through
even the darkest hours I'll face.
AMEN.

PART TWO

WORKING
IT
OUT

TEN

WORKING FOR A WORTHY CAUSE

You yourselves know how you ought to follow our example. We were not idle when we were with you, nor did we eat anyone's food without paying for it. On the contrary, we worked night and day, laboring and toiling so that we would not be a burden to any of you.

2 Thessalonians 3:7-8

Elaine, who is a sixth-grade teacher, esti-
mates that she corrects about 7,000
papers every school year.

Tricia, who is the receptionist for an insur-
ance firm, figures she answers over 1,100
phone calls a month.

Sue, the marketing manager for a large
company, found that she compiled nearly 300
pages' worth of reports every year.

Do these figures represent the sum total
of these women's work? When you and I
spend almost 50 percent of our waking hours
either on the job or going to and from work,
is that what we have to show for it—papers
and phone calls?

Of course not. Work, whether it is waiting on tables or making multi-million dollar

decisions, has a much more important role in God's world—and our lives—than that.

Scripture clearly validates the importance of work. The psalmist prayed, "May the favor of the Lord our God rest upon us; establish the work of our hands for us—yes, establish the work of our hands" (Psalm 90:17). Work is one way we put to use the resources God has given us—time, health, physical and mental capabilities. Work enables us to meet our material needs, to practice discipline, and to learn good stewardship of our time and talent. Proverbs emphasizes, "One who is slack in his work is brother to one who destroys" (18:9).

The work setting is a special mission field. A woman I know, Grace, works in a Christian company. She was distressed recently when a coworker commented on her friendship with one of her customers, Bev. "Some of us around the office think you're spending too much time with Bev," the coworker said. "After all, she's not a Christian. Everybody knows what kind of lifestyle she has."

Bev was a successful and slightly flamboyant businesswoman whose romantic escapades kept the office gossip mill occupied. She and Grace had lunch together frequently, and Bev often invited Grace to her company's functions.

Grace was hurt and surprised by her coworker's remark. She liked Bev, and she felt that their friendship had caused Bev to reflect on her own values and choices.

"Because I'm a Christian, am I supposed to avoid nonChristians?" Grace asked later in frustration. "Didn't Jesus spend time with tax collectors and prostitutes? I thought He taught us to reach out to those who don't know Him. Would I be a better Christian if I told her, 'I'm sorry, I can't be your friend because I don't like your lifestyle'?"

In most workplaces, Christian values and standards of behavior are the exception, not the rule. Many of our coworkers or customers, like Bev, may not even be acquainted with other Christians. They measure what it means to be a Christian by what they see in us. When we exercise our Christian faith, whether by choosing not to gossip or arguing against unethical practices, we are witnessing to others.

Our work gives us unique opportunities to do God's work. Let's go back to our friends at the beginning of the chapter. Earlier we asked about the sum total of their work. If it's not measured in papers and phone calls, how is it measured? How about by its impact on others' lives?

Each year Elaine has twenty-five students

in her class—twenty-five young minds and hearts that will be influenced by her example. Her love, concern, and discipline will shape their thinking and their values. What better place for Christ to be seen through her?

Tricia has hundreds of chances to make a difference in the lives of others by her pleasant, helpful attitude on the phone or a friendly greeting in the office lobby. We've all had days made brighter by a kind word or gesture from a total stranger, and most often they don't even know the impact they've had on us.

Sue, as the manager of a department, sets the tone for the people she supervises. It's not her 300 pages of reports that represents the value of her work. It's the example she sets for those around her: handling authority with fairness and compassion; cultivating the best in others, instead of trying to make sure they don't outshine her; showing patience and self-control under pressure.

No matter what work you do, it gives you the opportunity to be Christ's ambassador to those with whom you come in contact. Jesus wants you to "let your light shine before men, that they may see your good deeds and praise your Father in heaven" (Matthew 5:16). Where are the opportunities for you to light up your workplace?

❧**PRAYER**❧

*Father God, please give me the insight to see
the true value in my everyday work.
Help me to see beyond the paycheck
and the paperwork,
to discover what important work
I can do for You in my workplace.*
AMEN.

ELEVEN

WRONG PLACE, WRONG TIME

Blessed is the man who perseveres under trial, because when he has stood the test, he will receive the crown of life that God has promised to those who love him.

James 1:12

TODAY'S TO-DO LIST

☙ Learn how to cope with days when my body is at work but my mind is at home

W e've all had them: those days when, on the list of places we don't want to be, work is at the top.

Your twelve-year-old son complained of a stomachache this morning, but you sent him to school anyway, knowing the chances are fifty-fifty that (1) his ailment is real or (2) he has a math test today.

Your sixteen-year-old daughter just got her driver's license and insisted on bringing you to work so that she could use your car after school. She's in the throes of breaking up with her boyfriend. There's no telling what her plans for the car could be.

Your mother hasn't been feeling well and is going for her checkup at 11:00 today, and you're worried.

All in all, this isn't your favorite day to be at work.

Working mothers grow accustomed to feeling that they should be home when they're at work and at work when they're at home, but some days that conflict feels stronger than others: When a child is ill. When an argument with your spouse is unresolved. When the family is in a crisis. When a loved one or friend needs your support. Some of the time, we can take days off and be where we need to be; other times, we can't. How do we survive those days when we seem to be in the wrong place at the wrong time?

Head off guilt before it gains a foothold. You haven't done anything wrong. Going to work when the home front needs your attention doesn't mean you're choosing your job over your family. You're simply fulfilling conflicting obligations in the best way you can. Anyone who's been in the workplace knows you have to be judicious in how you allocate your sick and vacation days; otherwise, when there's a real emergency you'll be in a jam.

If you've prayed about and evaluated the situation and decided to go to work, let the decision rest. Remember, too, that you didn't cause any of the things that are going on at home: your mother's poor health, your son's stomachache/math anxiety, or your daughter's teenage traumas. You're doing the best you can. Give yourself credit for that.

Don't be contagious. Misery does indeed love company, but don't look for it at work. Your bosses and coworkers won't thank you for sharing your mood by biting their heads off when they ask you a question, moping around the office, or failing to do your share of the workload. Discuss your concerns with a friend at break time, not with the whole office.

Keep your finger on the domestic pulse. You'll feel better if you know what's going on. Call your mother on your lunch hour and ask about her doctor's appointment. Check in with the after-school care center and see how your son is feeling. Call home to see if your daughter is there, and if so, ask what her plans are. Don't waste work time on extended conversations; just touch base to reassure yourself no crises have erupted. Then refocus your mind on work.

Tackle a project you're dreading. It may sound crazy, but look at it this way: Your day is already off to a bad start, so tackling a task you don't like isn't going to make it any worse. And think how good you'll feel when it's done! Besides, the more concentration the task requires, the less you'll worry about what's happening at home.

Remind yourself that you're not alone.

Ask the Holy Spirit for a sense of peace. Entrust your loved ones to His care. Share the load with Him.

God understands what we're feeling on these wrong place/wrong time days, and He also knows that we're doing the best we can. One quality that makes Christ such a life-changing Savior is that He knows exactly what it's like to be human. "For we do not have a high priest who is unable to sympathize with our weaknesses, but we have one who has been tempted in every way, just as we are—yet was without sin" (Hebrews 4:15).

Days like this have all kinds of temptations: to focus so much on our own concerns that we run roughshod over the feelings of others; to try to make others feel inadequate because we're feeling inadequate ourselves; to let preoccupations keep us from giving those around us our full attention; to give our employer less than our best effort. Days like this challenge us to muster, along with everything else, a healthy dose of old-fashioned self-discipline and perseverance.

We all have bad days, but we never face them alone. God is ready to listen: "Let us then approach the throne of grace with confidence, so that we may receive mercy and find grace to help us in our time of need" (Hebrews 4:16).

❧PRAYER❧

*God, I thank You
that You understand these days
when I feel so torn by the demands
of my work and home life.
Give me Your peace. I know that, although I
can't be in two places at once, You can.*

AMEN.

TWELVE

TRUST ME, DEAR

*While [Jesus] was still speaking
a crowd came up, and the man who was
called Judas, one of the Twelve, was
leading them. He approached Jesus
to kiss him, but Jesus asked him,
"Judas, are you betraying the Son of Man
with a kiss?"*
Luke 22:47-48

TODAY'S TO-DO LIST

✒ Reflect on ways that I unintentionally deceive or disappoint those who trust me

Sandy's coworker Arlene needs to ask Sandy for a favor.

"I'm supposed to go to the employee council meeting Tuesday after work," Arlene says, "but my son has a championship baseball game that night at 6:00 and I really, really want to go. Would you mind going to the meeting for me? I'll be glad to cover a meeting for you sometime to make it up to you."

"No problem. I don't have any plans for that night anyway," Sandy says. "I'll be glad to go."

Later in the week, Sandy is talking with another coworker, Fran.

"I wish Arlene would take care of her own responsibilities instead of pushing them off on me," Sandy complains. "Why can't she go to the meeting herself? If she has to miss her son's ball game, that's just too bad. I have a life, too. I don't know why she thinks I have all this free time to waste doing things she's supposed to do."

The next morning, Fran passes Arlene in the coffee room. "You'd better steer clear of Sandy!" she jokes. "She's pretty worked up about having to go to that meeting for you."

Arlene is flabbergasted. Sandy certainly didn't give her any indication that she didn't want to cover the meeting, but now she's complaining to other people about it. Arlene feels hurt, embarrassed, and disappointed in Sandy, who she thought was a friend. She would rather have missed her son's ball game than caused Sandy to be upset with her. *Why,* Arlene wonders, *didn't Sandy tell me that she didn't want to take my place at the meeting?*

Most of us have had an experience like this at some time. Someone turns out not to be as loyal, or as trustworthy, or as much of a friend as we thought, and it hurts. We feel betrayed. Or maybe we're the ones who have let someone else down, and their sense of disappointment and betrayal hurts us, too.

What causes these "small betrayals" that we commit in everyday life?

Personal gain is one cause. While most of

us aren't likely to be offered huge bribes by cigar-wielding gangsters, we still commit small betrayals for personal gain of one kind or another. We gossip about a friend's marital problems, told to us in confidence, to impress others with our inside knowledge. We criticize our coworkers to the boss to make our own performance look better. We betray our employer's trust by saying negative things about the company or by using our work hours for non-work activities.

Insincerity is another factor that often causes others to feel betrayed by us. Insincerity is an "act as though" proposition. Sandy acted as though she were a good friend to Arlene, but when Arlene's back was turned, she criticized and complained.

How often are we guilty of "acting as though"?

We put on a show of working hard and doing a good job as long as the boss is around, but when she's away we declare an extended coffee break.

We act as though we're happy to accept a responsibility for our church or club, then we gripe and moan about what a burden it is.

We act as though we're proud of our spouse's promotion or his kitchen remodeling job, then we mutter to a neighbor that the new job doesn't pay well enough or the kitchen isn't the way we wanted it.

Additionally, our own small betrayals sometimes stem from a self-centered focus that extends only to our own needs and desires. We either don't consider the potential effect of our actions on someone else, or we simply don't care. Sandy didn't give any thought to how her remarks could affect Arlene—who was bound to hear them via the office grapevine.

Whether it's betraying a spouse through infidelity, or betraying a friend through a cruel remark, we betray Christ as well when we let untrustworthiness and deceit become part of our lives.

The Bible tells us that one of Judah's rulers, King Amaziah, "did what was right in the eyes of the LORD, but not wholeheartedly" (2 Chronicles 25:2). Maybe that's the most common betrayal of all: doing the right thing, but for the wrong reasons.

Perhaps we can be less inclined to betray others if we remember the words of advice that King David gave to his son: "You, my son Solomon, acknowledge the God of your father, and serve him with wholehearted devotion and with a willing mind, for the LORD searches every heart and understands every motive behind the thoughts" (1 Chronicles 28:9).

☙PRAYER☙

*Dear Lord, I want to live honestly
with those around me.
Teach me discretion in the things I say
and do, so that others can trust me
to be the person they believe me to be.
May I discipline my heart
to never intentionally
deceive or betray.*
AMEN.

THIRTEEN

I SEE,
I SEE!

*"For this people's heart has become
calloused; they hardly hear with their ears,
and they have closed their eyes.
Otherwise they might see with their eyes,
hear with their ears, understand with their
hearts and turn, and I would heal them."*

Matthew 13:15

TODAY'S TO-DO LIST

❧ Practice not only looking at, but seeing, what is within and around me

Sheila needs new sneakers for her aerobics class tonight, so during her lunch hour she runs into a discount store that recently opened near her office. She dashes over to the center aisle and looks up and down, but can't find the shoe department.

She grabs the nearest store employee. "Where are the shoes?" she asks hurriedly, as her lunch hour ticks away.

The salesperson points. "Down this aisle, on the left," she says, "right under the sign."

Sheila looks up. There, in three-foot high, red letters on a sign hanging from the ceiling, it says "SHOES."

"Oh," she says sheepishly, "I see now."

Like Sheila, we are people who "have eyes to see but do not see" (Ezekiel 12:2). We look at those around us but we can't see their needs, their unique qualities, or what makes them do the things they do. We look at the difficult decisions we have to make but we can't see God's will in our lives. We look at ourselves in the mirror but we can't see what's going on inside; sometimes we don't even know what we really want or why we want it. What causes our poor vision?

Blurry priorities. Right now, this very minute, could you write down the five most important priorities in your life? In order to stay on course toward the critical goals in our lives, we must know at any given moment what our priorities are.

God's commands are a clear guide in setting priorities. We are to love and serve Him. We are to love others as ourselves. We are to teach God's commands to our children and keep Christ's example before them. We are to care for the needy. How those guidelines translate into day-to-day living is different for each of us.

Take a moment now—or at least some time today—to jot down your primary goal for each important aspect of your life: (1) marriage; (2) parenthood; (3) work; (4) self/personal growth; (5) social/community roles. When we know what our priorities are, we are able to make decisions that will support them, not work against them. We see our way more clearly when we have God-confirmed priorities to guide us.

Cloudy compassion. In our humanness, our view of other people is often clouded. We see others through the screen of our own needs and experiences rather than with the clear-eyed compassion of Christ.

For example, there's Charlotte, a woman who might work in any office. You and I see a bitter, negative, hard-driven woman who'll do anything to get ahead. Rumor has it that anything you say in front of her goes right to the boss's ear if she thinks it'll work in her favor. She'll brag to you endlessly about her smart, talented kids, but don't bother to tell her about yours, because she's not interested.

If we could clear away our own prejudices and insecurities, and look at Charlotte through eyes of compassion, what would we see? We'd see a lonely, frightened woman whose painful divorce left her feeling battered and rejected. She's desperately afraid of losing her job and being unable to support her children, so she'll do whatever it takes to stay in the boss's good graces. She feels so unloved and unlovable that she can't imagine anyone wanting to be her friend. And she's so burdened by her own concerns that she hasn't the time or energy to share anyone else's.

Not everyone has a personality we enjoy or is cut out to be our best friend. However, when we look at others in terms of their needs and their private hurts rather than our own, we often gain insights that both help and heal.

Distorted perspective. Remember those wavy mirrors in the funhouse at the county fair? They could make you look as round as a bowling ball, or as tall and skinny as a drinking straw.

Our inner vision of ourselves can become distorted like this, too. We compare ourselves to a glamorous model or a wildly successful businesswoman, and we feel frumpy and incompetent. We attend a social function and worry that people won't like us because we're too shy or too talkative or too unsophisticated or too serious, because someone else once told us that we were. We want to please others, but feel that we never quite measure up to their expectations.

Our vision becomes distorted when we look at ourselves only in terms of others' expectations or the world's standards. God, on the other hand, sees us as uniquely ourselves, created and equipped to serve Him as only we can. The jumble of positive and negative qualities within us brings its own unique challenges as we seek to live daily by Christ's example.

If we want others to see Christ in us, we must learn first of all to see Him in ourselves. That's 20/20 vision.

✥PRAYER✥

Lord God, please give me better spiritual vision. Make my priorities clear and help me to view both myself and others as You would in the light of Your love.
AMEN.

FOURTEEN

WHAT A DEAL!

*Jesus entered the temple area
and drove out all who were buying
and selling there. . . .
"It is written," he said to them,
"'My house will be called a house
of prayer,' but you are making it
a 'den of robbers.'"*

Matthew 21:12-13

TODAY'S TO-DO LIST

🖎 Teach my children by my example
   that not everything of value is
   measured in dollars

NEWS FLASH! "George J. Bigman, president of XYZ Enterprises, recently
announced plans to purchase the
island of Guam for development into a private
vacation getaway. Bigman is rumored to have
a personal net worth of over $172 million."

Isn't it frightening that we take the phrase
"personal net worth" and express it in dollars,
as though a person were a microwave oven in
an appliance sale?

We live in a world obsessed with money,
with the transactions of buying and selling.
From the very earliest age, our children are
sent the message that everything in life is a
transaction. Buy our breakfast cereal and we'll
give you a free frisbee. Give me the cookies
from your lunch and I'll be your best friend.

No wonder it's hard to teach our children values like volunteerism, sacrificial giving, loyalty, and forgiveness. No wonder it's hard to convince them that we'll love them regardless of their grades or their athletic performance or their musical talent. Unconditional love doesn't fit the buying/selling model.

At a community function a few years ago, I was introduced to a local business executive.

"What kind of work do you do?" he immediately asked me.

"I'm a writer," I said. "I write books."

"Mmm-hmm," he said, looking thoughtful. "Is there any money in that?"

The theory goes that if it doesn't pay a lot of money, it's not worth doing. People are viewed as eccentric if they pursue jobs because they are meaningful or satisfying or humanitarian rather than lucrative.

A spinoff of this buy/sell philosophy is that it's essential to drive a hard bargain, to wring the highest return out of the lowest investment. Now, when it comes to shopping, all of us have to bargain hunt; that's the kind of economy we live in. But bargain hunting in other areas of life is destructive and out of keeping with the principle of genuine commitment.

Do we rear spiritually healthy, responsible, well-adjusted children by seeing how little time and energy we can invest in them? Do we build a loving, lasting marriage by being just faithful enough to keep it together? Are we dealing honestly with our employers when we see how little work we can do and still bring home our paycheck?

Several years ago, after a great deal of work and study, I passed an accreditation exam in the field of public relations. Having passed the exam, I was then allowed to use the professional designation "APR" after my name.

Eventually I received a notice in the mail from the national PR organization, which had sponsored the exam, saying that it was time for me to pay my annual dues. The three-figure fee was more than I thought I could spend, so I decided to let my membership expire.

Later, when I was talking to the president of the local chapter, he mentioned that my membership renewal hadn't come across his desk. I told him I wasn't going to renew.

"You lose the APR designation, then," he said. "You can't use it after your name anymore."

Okay. I didn't pay my dues, so I was out of the club. And if you don't pay your light bill, the power company turns off your electricity. It makes sense: Organizations and companies need money to operate. Yet we need to be sure we don't live by the same philosophy.

If a child strays from the course I desire for him, I don't kick him out of the family or turn off my love. If a friend hasn't invited me out for lunch in a long time, I don't scratch her off my list. If my church's Sunday school program isn't run exactly the way I think it should be, I don't quit attending or giving. Nonpayment of dues by others doesn't give us permission to throw them out of the club or cut them off from our love, loyalty, or friendship.

How do we teach our children that not everything in life operates in the buying/selling mode? Primarily by our example.

My friend Kim was surprised recently when her six-year-old daughter came up to her with a handful of change. "I want to send this to those hungry children I saw on TV," she said.

Kim and her daughter had never talked specifically about the importance of giving money to charity, but Kim's involvement in and support of local charities apparently conveyed a message.

"I guess I must be doing something right," Kim told me later.

I guess so, too.

❦PRAYER❧

*Lord, thank You for all that You have given
me. Strengthen me to stand against
the forces of materialism
and acquisitiveness. Please guide me
as I seek to teach my children
that Your grace, like love, is not for sale.*
AMEN.

FIFTEEN

CUT YOUR LOSSES

*People who want to get rich fall
into temptation and a trap
and into many foolish and harmful
desires that plunge men into ruin
and destruction.*

1 Timothy 6:9

TODAY'S TO-DO LIST

- Cultivate an attitude of contentment
- Resist striving for material gain as an end in itself

When my husband's longtime friend Charlie visited us one weekend, the three of us went to an estate auction held at an old farmhouse out in the country. All the furnishings and other contents of the house were to be auctioned.

I entered the bidding on an antique mirror with a beautiful frame that would have looked perfect in my front hallway. However, a very persistent antique dealer kept bidding against me until the price was way beyond what I could pay for the mirror.

On the way home, I lamented being outbid for the mirror. I had pictured it in my hallway as though I already had it. "I'm really disappointed about that mirror," I kept saying.

Charlie, who was a veteran auction-goer,

said, "Well, I look at it this way. Sure, you wanted the mirror, but since you never had it in the first place, it's not like you've lost anything."

We haven't seen Charlie in over ten years, but his insightful remark has stayed with me. It seems to speak clearly to a common attitude about material possessions.

When we lose something or someone—a loved one dies, our home is burglarized, we're laid off a job—there is a gap in our lives. Where there used to be a presence, there's now an empty space. We feel a genuine sense of loss; that thing or person is gone. Every day, we are reminded of our loss by seeing or feeling that empty spot in our homes, in our schedules, or in our families.

Our commercialism-crazed culture fosters a similar sense of loss, but over things we never had. It portrays a happy life as one filled with a vast array of splendid things—a decorated dream home, up-to-the-minute wardrobe, gleaming new car, glamorous vacations, and on and on and on. When we deeply desire a certain material acquisition and can't obtain it, we feel a sense of loss. Even though we never actually had it, we feel it's been taken away.

Every now and then a celebrity, being quoted about his or her background, will say something like, "My family was poor, but we didn't know it, so we were happy." Living in our buying-obsessed culture is just the opposite; we view ourselves as poor and deprived only because we're constantly shown all the things we don't have. And it makes us unhappy.

Going through our lives with this sense of being cheated and deprived blocks our joy in daily living and stunts our Christian growth. When we feel ourselves falling into that trap, it's time to redirect our thinking.

The first thing we need is a shift in focus. Advertisers spend billions of dollars each year to create consumer demand for products we don't need and can't afford. We are being manipulated into focusing on what we don't have rather than on what we do have.

All it takes to move our focus back on track is reminding ourselves that people in many parts of the world, even in our own country, would gratefully eat the garbage we scrape off our dinner plates. There are families for whom the idea of wearing new, unused clothing is a fantasy, totally out of reach, families for whom owning a car or a TV set is as remote as owning a spaceship. A reality check can do wonders for restoring both our perspective and our thankfulness.

Another self-reminder that helps us resist

the cultural tide of materialism is this: Having material possessions to satisfy our desires is *not* a God-given right. Our inheritance is a spiritual one, not a material one. We start with nothing. Anything we have, we have not because we are entitled to it but because it is a gift from God. And we know that "from everyone who has been given much, much will be demanded" (Luke 12:48). God's Word gives us clear instructions about using our worldly resources for His Kingdom rather than for our own desires.

Finally, God offers us freedom from the constant, wearisome striving for more material gain. We seize that freedom when we cultivate an attitude of contentment. The Bible reminds us, "Godliness with contentment is great gain. For we brought nothing into the world, and we can take nothing out of it. But if we have food and clothing, we will be content with that" (1 Timothy 6:6-8).

Notice that, according to Paul's letter to Timothy, contentment has a spiritual companion: godliness. Godliness, or devotion to God's commands, gives us the eternal perspective that allows us to learn contentment. Contentment, in turn, gives us peace and freedom from striving. Contentment is neither laziness nor bondage to the status quo, but rather a deep-down satisfaction unrelated to what we do or don't possess.

Let's stop grieving over things we never had and rejoice in the incredible gift we have been given: the gift of life, both present and eternal.

❧PRAYER❧

*God, I want to accept Your freedom
from striving for material gain.
Create a spirit of contentment in me.
Teach me not only to be thankful for what
I do possess, but to share it according
to Your commands.*
AMEN.

SIXTEEN

CALL IN THE CLEANUP CREW

*Do everything without complaining
or arguing, so that you may become
blameless and pure, children of God
without fault in a crooked and depraved
generation, in which you shine like
stars in the universe as you hold out
the word of life.*

Philippians 2:14-16

Florida, my home state, is best known for
its beaches, but its attractions also
include some incredibly beautiful fresh-
water springs. My family and I visited one of
these springs a few years ago.

We took a tour boat ride along a quiet,
narrow river, with water so clear that we
could easily make out every pebble and plant
along the bottom. The tour guide explained
that the reason the water was so clear was
that it was freer from impurities than the
drinking water in most cities!

When we reached the spring, we could
see all the way down to where a steady flow of
tiny bubbles marked its opening. I was awe-
struck when the tour guide went on to say
that we were viewing the source of the spring

through *eighty feet* of water. I couldn't believe it. I was looking through eighty feet of water so pure that I could see the river bottom as clearly as if it were a foot away.

When I read the Bible's instruction for us to live lives of purity, I think of that beautiful, clear water, and I wonder if that's the essence of God's desire for His people: for us to live lives so pure that people around us can see clearly into our minds and hearts, see our every motive, every thought, every desire, and we have nothing to hide.

How would you feel if, right now, your family members, coworkers, fellow church members, and friends could see right into your heart? Would you be happy for them to see everything that's there? If you're like me, the answer is no.

What causes the impurities, the murky motives that cloud our lives, and how can we clean them up?

My eye doctor recently fitted me for a new pair of contact lenses. He explained that this type of lens is gas-permeable, meaning that they allow a healthy flow of oxygen to the surface of the eye. However, this same property also causes them to absorb substances from the environment, like gases in fumes and other pollutants. For that reason, he said, it's extremely important to clean them meticulously and regularly so that they don't transfer harmful substances to my eyes.

I believe that our hearts and minds "absorb" destructive elements from our environment, too, and these elements cause the murkiness that stands between us and a pure life. Elements like:

- The constant barrage of sexually oriented TV shows, commercials, movies, books, and magazine articles that foster a disregard for any limitations on sexual activity.

- The workplace mania that seeks money, power, accomplishment, status, recognition, and rewards without counting the cost.

- The world's obsession with appearances, the conviction that the image is more important than the substance, the belief that how you are seen by others is more important than who you are.

These and other destructive elements can be "absorbed" into our daily living without our even being aware of it unless we do two things: (1) Monitor and control our exposure to these elements; and (2) diligently "clean" our inner selves with a disciplined devotional life.

I believe this means being very discriminating in what type of material we watch, listen to, and read. It means seeking out leisure activities and friends that will build us up in Christ, not those that foster a worldly mindset. It also means being alert to sexual temptation; recognizing that what we insist is "just friendship" or a "good working relationship" often becomes something else no matter how adamantly we deny it.

Keeping ourselves pure also means making all our goals in life secondary to the one primary goal of serving the Lord. If we place our desires—for job advancement, or material gain, or accomplishment—all within the context of using them in the service of God's Kingdom, then we keep them in perspective. When they become only tools, they are no longer ends in themselves.

By constantly checking our own motives and asking ourselves, "Why am I doing this?" we work toward avoiding making choices on the basis of appearance rather than God's commands. After all, the only image that matters is the image of Christ that others see in us. When we seek to live lives of greater purity, others are able to see that image more and more clearly—maybe even from eighty feet away!

❧PRAYER❧

Dear God, I want to lead a pure life.
Give me the insight to see the impurities
and work at removing them.
Grant me the courage and the self-discipline
to say "no" to the sources
of impurity around me.
AMEN.

SEVENTEEN

I'M TAKING CARE OF BUSINESS —BUT WHOSE?

*Make it your ambition
to lead a quiet life,
to mind your own business.*

1 Thessalonians 4:11

TODAY'S TO-DO LIST

- ❧ Practice self-control when I'm tempted to gossip about others
- ❧ Look for ways to help other people when they have problems rather than talk about them

Television soap operas seem to have been with us as long as TV has. Here's a typical plot: Thelma suspects that her husband, Jake, is having an affair with his young secretary, Zondra who, in turn, is worried that she might be pregnant. She is, as Thelma suspects, having an affair with Jake, but she's also been seeing her old boyfriend, Joel, who just got out of jail after serving time for selling drugs. Joel, however, is obsessed with finding his long-lost sister, Adrienne, who was separated from him when they were sent to different foster homes as children. Little does he know that Adrienne was later adopted by Thelma and Jake. And so on.

For some reason, we are fascinated with other people's problems. Whether in real life or in soap operas, we are much more interested in what's going wrong in people's lives than what's going right.

A few weeks ago I overheard two women in a restaurant comparing notes on their favorite soap opera. They were having fun speculating on the various story lines—whether Herb or Dash was the father of Andrea's baby and whether Sandra would figure out that she was really Ellen's daughter, not her younger sister.

Maybe this is one reason soap operas remain so popular. They give us the chance to gossip freely about scandal and intrigue and to speculate wildly about the lives of others with no consequences.

Real life, of course, isn't like that. Other people's tragedies, weaknesses, and secrets aren't ours to gossip about, speculate on, analyze, or gloat over. But we do.

Why? Maybe it's because, seen through the eyes of our lower nature, the weaknesses and failures of others make our own seem less awful. We feel superior when something happens to someone else but we're "above" it. A part of us might even rejoice a little. We're pleased that the score is being evened, that the other person is not ahead of us in the quest for happiness. And when we gossip about others, it gives us the powerful feeling that we have an inside track on important information.

When looked at through the eyes of Christ, though, the trials of others take on a whole different light. They are opportunities to witness for Him by reaching out to a hurting person—to listen compassionately, to give a word of encouragement, to pray, to advise without judging, to lighten a burden by allowing it to be shared. When a friend or co-worker's problems become the coffee-break or backyard-fence topic of gossip, we have the chance to inject a positive note or to quell a rumor.

The Bible admonishes us to mind our own business and to avoid the temptations of gossip. By gossiping, the Bible says, we betray confidences, stir up dissension, separate friends, and feed quarrels. Gossip damages the reputations of others and demeans us in the process. As Paul pointed out, "Not only do they become idlers, but also gossips and busybodies, saying things they ought not to" (1 Timothy 5:13).

Wouldn't it be satisfying if we could help change this lunchtime conversation from this . . .

"Did you see Traci waltz in this morning showing off her new outfit? But just wait; you can bet that she'll gain back all that weight she lost on her diet."

"No kidding. Hey, did you hear that Jenny thinks her husband is going to get laid off from his job?"

"Maybe that's why she butters up the boss so much by turning in her work before it's due and staying so late when we're doing the end-of-the-month surveys."

"Do you think she could be staying late so often because she's having an affair with you-know-who?"

. . . into this?

"Doesn't Traci look beautiful in that outfit she wearing? That color of blue is so perfect for her."

"Sure does look good on her. You know, she has such a sweet personality. I love working with her."

"Speaking of personality, Jenny sure has seemed down in the dumps lately. I don't know what's bothering her, but I thought I'd ask her if she needed any help filing last month's invoices. That's such a huge job, and it can get pretty boring."

"That would be really nice. Let me know if you need any help."

Minding our own business mean's minding God's business. And His business is healing hurts, not spreading them. Let's make that our business, too.

❧PRAYER❧

*God, I don't know why the temptation
to gossip is so strong. I know it's not right,
but sometimes other people's problems
reassure me that mine aren't so bad.
Help me to be Christ's ambassador to the
hurting, not the rumor mill's power station.*
AMEN.

PART THREE

HOLDING DOWN THE HOME FRONT

EIGHTEEN

CHECK YOUR BAGGAGE AT THE DOOR

Consider it pure joy, my brothers,
whenever you face trials of many kinds,
because you know that the testing of your
faith develops perseverance.

James 1:2-3

TODAY'S TO-DO LIST

✍ Discipline myself not to let work problems intrude on my home life

D riving home from work, Bonnie is so angry she thinks steam could come out of her ears. In a meeting at work that day involving managers from several departments, Bonnie's boss, Carolyn, presented a list of proposed ideas for reorganizing the bookkeeping department. The ideas were all enthusiastically received and earned Carolyn compliments from the other managers.

Unfortunately, all the ideas were originally Bonnie's; she'd suggested them to Carolyn a few weeks earlier in an informal conversation. But in today's meeting, Carolyn never gave any indication that the ideas had come from anyone but herself.

Reviewing the day's events as she drives home, Bonnie can feel her anger and resentment reaching the boiling point. She's about five minutes away from the daycare center where she picks up the kids.

❧

Sounds like Bonnie is about to experience some job-to-home spillover—an occurrence familiar to almost any working mother: Upsetting events at work cause us to travel home at the end of the day with a load of negative feelings which, in turn, affect the way we deal with our families.

When we're faced with a situation like Bonnie's, how can we keep from taking out the day's frustrations on our unsuspecting loved ones?

Make a transition. Use the trip from work to the daycare center as a transition time to cool down and set aside the work-related baggage. Remind yourself that your kids didn't cause the problems at work and shouldn't have to pay the consequences. Count slowly to twenty-five, willing yourself to calm down and set aside your anger and agitation.

Before you arrive to pick up the kids, ask the Holy Spirit for peace and patience. Whatever kind of day you've had, the kids will still act like kids.

If you have enough time en route, try this short-term decision-making process: Identify *one step* you are going to take to deal with the problem. Commit to taking that step tomorrow and not stewing over the problem any more between now and then. You can always change your decision later, but this way you can set the problem aside for the time being with at least some sense of resolution.

"Just say no" to your mind. Your brain may want to keep sneaking back to whatever subject is troubling you. Be firm with yourself. When you feel your thoughts slipping in that direction, start talking to your spouse or kids about something else or simply change the focus of your thoughts.

If you feel a strong need to talk about it with someone, choose a specific time to do so later in the evening, with your spouse or a friend, but confine the discussion to that period rather than dwelling on it all evening. Returning repeatedly to the problem will only stir up your feelings again and create a stressful evening instead of a relaxing one.

Simplify the evening. If you can afford it, this is a good night to go out for hamburgers instead of fixing dinner. Keep the evening as stress-free as possible. Exercise if you can. Activity helps drain off the emotional energy and tension that have accumulated during the day.

Keep the lid on. Tonight may be the night your teenage son announces that "all his friends are going" to a concert this weekend and he wants to go, too. You know there's a battle ahead, since you've had this conversation before. If possible, postpone the discussion until a later time. Tell him the truth: You've had a rough day and feel you can't approach the subject with an open mind.

If there's no time for a twenty-four-hour postponement, ask your son to come back in fifteen minutes to discuss it. Use that time to collect your thoughts and decide how you want to handle the situation. If your spouse is involved, discuss it with him so you can present a unified stance with your son. Taking this time to prepare will help you avoid suddenly dumping the day's frustrations on the table if the discussion gets heated.

Hand it over. Turn the problem over to the Holy Spirit. Take time to ask for guidance, wisdom, and compassion. Ask for freedom from the burdensome emotions that you are still carrying from your day at work. Let Christ relieve you of the weight.

The members of our families are among God's most precious blessings to us. Leaving our work problems on the doorstep is one of the most difficult skills that working mothers are challenged to master. Thank God that He has given us His Spirit and is ready and willing to help!

❧PRAYER❧

*Dear God, it seems like I have so little time
with my family members—
between the demands of my job,
their activities, and other commitments.
Don't let me spoil our time together
by bringing home negative emotions
and feelings from work.
Grant me the discipline and skills
to check my baggage at the door.*
AMEN.

NINETEEN

PACK THAT SUITCASE CAREFULLY

Fix these words of mine in your hearts and minds. . . .
Teach them to your children, talking about them when you sit at home and when you walk along the road, when you lie down and when you get up.

Deuteronomy 11:18-19

TODAY'S TO-DO LIST

ᗢ Make decisions now about what values I want my children to carry with them in the future
ᗢ Work at equipping my children with these values through example and instruction

Any mother who has ever taken a long trip with children knows the challenge of keeping the kids entertained. One way that my family has whiled away a lot of travel time is by playing "I'm Going on a Trip."

Basically, the game goes like this: The first player says, "I'm going on a trip. In my suitcase, I'm going to pack a toothbrush."

The second player repeats the statement, with the addition of another item, saying, "I'm going on a trip. In my suitcase, I'm going to pack a toothbrush and a pair of pajamas."

The third player then adds another item to the list: "I'm going on a trip. In my suitcase, I'm going to pack a toothbrush, a pair of pajamas, and an alarm clock." And so on. The hard part, of course, is simply remembering all the items as the list grows longer and longer.

As mothers, one of our most important tasks is to pack a spiritual suitcase for our children, so that when they leave our homes they will have what they need for their continuing journey through life. We start this packing when they are babies; we give them a sense of being loved, a firm sense of security and belonging.

As they grow into children, we add items to the suitcase: We teach them what it means to be a Christian; we foster a basic sense of moral values based on God's commands. We teach them to share, to care about others, to behave responsibly. In preparation for adolescence, we add items like the importance of standing up for what is right, accepting responsibility for our own actions, and understanding consequences.

During the teenage years, we load the suitcase with reassurance of self-worth and reaffirmation of basic values. We double-check to make sure all those items we packed in previous years are still intact—because the child will be leaving us soon. A time will come when we no longer have the opportunity to add things to the suitcase; anything we've forgotten will have to be done without.

Have you ever had to make an overnight

trip on short notice, and found yourself grabbing things and throwing them into the suitcase without much thought? We can't really afford to take this last-minute, random approach to packing our children's spiritual luggage, but that often happens amid the clamor of other demands.

Worn out by time pressures, work tensions, and over-commitment, we're easily tempted to shortcut the time and effort needed to teach our children important life-lessons. Scolding and punishing are easier than constructive discipline. "Because I said so" is easier than a thoughtful explanation of why things are the way they are. But what do these parental shortcuts contribute to the contents of the child's suitcase?

Here's another common luggage problem: You arrive at your destination and find that all the clothes you brought are either too warm or not warm enough for the weather. In other words, what you've packed is inappropriate and won't be of any use. Are we equipping our children with values and skills that will truly serve them well when they enter the world of job choices, financial decisions, marriage, and homes of their own? Or are we giving them baggage that will turn out to be useless when they have to make important choices and build lasting relationships?

Are we showing them, for example, that you resolve problems by becoming angry or changing the subject? Are we loading their suitcases with ways to avoid responsibility and take the easy route instead of the right one?

And then there's always the lost-luggage trauma, in which you arrive at your destination but your luggage doesn't. What happens then? You make do with whatever you can to meet your basic needs. You borrow a few clothes from someone, buy a toothbrush, and improvise, wearing two borrowed sweatshirts and a rain jacket instead of the warm coat you had hoped to bring.

If we fail to provide our children with the luggage they need for effective Christian living, they'll do these same things when they're on their own: they'll borrow philosophies and beliefs from others; they'll replace sketchy former values with new ones, and they'll improvise—making choices based solely on circumstances. They'll have no suitcase to go back to, no tried-and-true value system on which to build their adult lives.

Maybe it's a good idea for us to play a little memory game with ourselves when we're driving to work or waiting for an appointment: "My child is going on a trip. In his suitcase, I'm going to pack: a sense of self-worth as a child of God . . . the basis for a firm commitment to Christ . . . a knowledge that he is loved unconditionally . . . sensitivity to the needs of others . . . willingness to go against the crowd if necessary. . . ."

❧PRAYER❧

Dear Father God,
You have entrusted my children to me
out of Your infinite grace and wisdom.
Guide me as I prepare and equip them
for living lives that will glorify You—
lives of deep-seated joy, enduring
compassion, and faithful service.
AMEN.

TWENTY

KANGAROO COURT IS NOW IN SESSION

Follow justice and justice alone, so that you may live and possess the land the LORD your God is giving you.

Deuteronomy 16:20

Yet the LORD longs to be gracious to you; he rises to show you compassion. For the LORD is a God of justice.

Isaiah 30:18

TODAY'S TO-DO LIST

☞ Cultivate the godly quality of justice by practicing fairness to myself as well as others

---

You're standing in a huge courtroom. A stern-looking judge is seated behind an enormous bench. Behind you a crowd of people creates a low hubbub in the room as they whisper and point at you.

"Silence!" the judge roars, and the crowd quiets down. "Now, what is this woman accused of?" he asks. You look around, wondering who's on trial, and you see to your astonishment that he's pointing at *you*.

A woman in the back of the room jumps up. You recognize her. She's your daughter's teacher.

"I accuse her of cookie counterfeiting!" the woman shouts. "When we had our third-grade Christmas party, *her* daughter Susie brought *store-bought* cookies. Little Katie

White's mother—a fine, religious woman—made reindeer-shaped cookies with chocolate sprinkles on the antlers. Why can't this woman be more like Mrs. White?"

"What do you have to say for yourself?" the judge asks you.

"There wasn't time to bake cookies that week," you stammer. "I'd had the flu so I was behind in all my housework and things were so hectic at the office, and I was just too tired the night before the party, and. . . ."

The judge slams a gavel the size of a sledgehammer down on his desk, shaking the whole room. "Guilty! Guilty! Guilty!" he roars. "What else is she accused of?"

A man stands up. "I accuse her of field-trip failure! We needed parents to drive the youth group to an all-day rally on Saturday—and she said she couldn't because her boss had put everyone on overtime all weekend. Sure, sure! What kind of mother is she?!"

"Well?" the judge says pointedly to you. "What do you have to say for yourself this time?"

"Nobody at work was getting time off that weekend, because . . ." you begin.

The gavel crashes down again. "Guilty! Guilty! Guilty!"

Another woman waves her arms frantically and jumps up. "I want to be heard, too!"

she says. "I'm an employee at the daycare center where her child goes, and I accuse her of daycare delinquency! Last Wednesday, she didn't pick up her child until nearly *six* o'clock!" A shocked murmur sweeps through the room. "When she finally got there, she rushed in with some story about car trouble on the way back from a meeting. Imagine!

"And I *heard*," she continues in a conspiratorial whisper, "that some nights she goes to an *aerobics* class instead of staying at home with her children. It's all so shocking," she adds, fanning herself as though she might faint.

This time the judge doesn't even give you a chance to speak. The gavel strikes again. "Guilty! Guilty! Guilty!"

"I've heard enough," the judge goes on. "I sentence you to feeling guilty all the time for the next twelve years or until all of your children have left home—whichever comes last."

Our kangaroo court seems pretty silly, doesn't it? And yet, I believe we convene this kind of court in our own minds every time we fail to meet a commitment or fulfill an expectation, whether it's ours or someone else's and whether it's a reasonable expectation or a totally unrealistic one.

We not only *feel* guilty; we actually convince ourselves that we *should* feel guilty. We convict ourselves of such pseudo-crimes as cookie counterfeiting, field-trip failure, and daycare delinquency. We hammer away with our internal gavels, telling ourselves we're "Guilty! Guilty! Guilty!"

Guilty of what? Of having only twenty-four hours in a day? Of having to fulfill job responsibilities? Of being subject to the hazards of car trouble, traffic delays, long meetings, and other realities we don't control? Of needing and wanting to take care of our own physical, mental, and spiritual well-being?

God instructs us to demonstrate justice and mercy, and surely the justice we extend to others must begin with the way we treat ourselves. Christ's death washed us clean of sins far more damaging than buying cookies and being late; we demean His sacrifice when we let the petty baggage of guilt burden us unnecessarily.

While all of us would like to be able to do more, the truth is that our children will survive without homemade cookies. They can cope with our being late or not being able to go on field trips. Our best gift to them is the assurance of Christ's love and our love and our own example that teaches justice for both ourselves and others.

❧PRAYER❧

Dear Savior, I work so hard,
but there always seems to be something
I should be doing that I'm not,
and I feel guilty about it.
Help me to practice justice for myself
and to accept Your gift of loving grace.
AMEN.

TWENTY-ONE

I WISH
I HAD
WINGS

He will cover you with his feathers,
and under his wings you will find refuge;
his faithfulness will be your shield
and rampart.

Psalm 91:4

TODAY'S TO-DO LIST

☙ Model my parenting role after the example God gives us as a loving Father

From time to time a women's magazine or a TV talk show will feature an interview with some "celebrity mom"—an actress, musician, journalist, or other well-known woman who talks about how hard it is to juggle her busy career with her family life. She bemoans the travel demanded by her job that takes her away from her children; she describes her efforts to schedule "quality time" with them, at home or on the road. She emphasizes how important her family life is to her and how much she makes it a priority in her schedule.

While these women are undoubtedly sincere in their desire to be good mothers, I think it's hard to identify with them. For one thing, they're paid more in salary each year than most of us earn in a decade. Their households include a flock of nannies, tutors, housekeepers, chauffeurs, hairdressers, and other helpers to make sure everything gets done. The rest of us are on our own, trying to make ends meet, equipped with a carpool schedule and a curling iron instead of a chauffeur and a hairdresser.

Where do today's working mothers look for role models, then? Obviously these celebrity moms don't fill the bill. Our own mothers and our friends all came into motherhood with just as little training as we had. Who can best teach us Motherhood 101?

Surely it isn't accidental that, when God entered into a new covenant with humankind, He chose a Parent-child relationship to be the basis of that covenant. While a father is not a mother, the principles of loving parenthood that God teaches us transcend the differences of gender.

Let's look at some of those principles.

Clear expectations. From the very beginning, God has spelled out His expectations of us. He established clear rules for how His people—His children—are to live. Can we do any less for our own children?

Child psychologists have told us for years that children need a consistent framework of rules and expectations in their environment;

it gives them a sense of security and assurance that we as their parents care about them. If we are vague about what we expect from our children and what rules we expect them to live by, then we shouldn't be surprised when they don't follow our expectations.

Freedom to choose. Free will is one hallmark of God's relationship with humankind. Over the centuries, men and women have caused an infinite amount of grief to God, to themselves, and to one another by the choices they've made.

Similarly, the choices our children make often aren't what we would choose for them, whether it's the choice of a hairstyle, the choice of what to do after high school, or the choice of a life partner. But the choice is still theirs. I believe one of our most critical goals as parents must be to give our children the skills and the values they need to make wise choices throughout life. And our best teaching technique for that particular course is to let them gain experience in decision-making. We can do this by pointing out possibilities instead of dictating choices.

Teaching by consequence. One necessary byproduct of free will is dealing with the consequences of our choices. When our children are small, often we have to intervene to keep them from danger—if they choose to cross the street in front of a car, we stop them rather than letting them be hurt. But as they grow older, we're challenged to let go more and more, giving them the freedom to choose and then the freedom to deal with the results of their choices.

Unconditional love. For some reason, my son loves to tease me by asking, "Would you still love me if I was a bank robber?" Maybe he just likes the reassurance of my answer, which is always the same: "I'll always love you, no matter what you do. I might be disappointed, or sorry about something you did, but I would still love you."

I believe that, even if we cannot achieve anything else as mothers, we must give our children that sense of refuge and security the psalmist talks about in Psalm 91:4.

We show our children what God's unconditional love is like by loving them unconditionally ourselves—not without discipline, not without consequences to deal with, but with no strings attached. We give them love that is not tied to their performance or their living up to our unfulfilled dreams or their making the same choices that we would have made.

Motherhood is one of those jobs that isn't for wimps. Praise God that we have not only

His Word and His guidance through the Holy Spirit, but also His example to help us prepare a new generation to worship and serve Him.

❧PRAYER❧

Dear heavenly Father,
parenthood is a sacred trust from You.
I'm so thankful that You are always
available to give me wisdom
and instruction. Bless my children, Lord;
please give them benefits from whatever I do
right as their mother, and don't allow them
to suffer too much from my mistakes.
AMEN.

TWENTY-TWO

THIS CALLS FOR A HANDS-ON APPROACH

Barak said to her,
"If you go with me, I will go;
but if you don't go with me, I won't go."
"Very well," Deborah said,
"I will go with you."

Judges 4:8-9

Jeanine has recently earned her real estate broker's license. The ink on her new business cards is barely dry, and she can't wait to make that first sale. She's sitting in her office, wearing a new suit, reading a magazine article about "Power Selling." She's ready!

The phone rings. It's a prospective buyer wanting to look at a house Jeanine has listed.

"Great!" Jeanine says enthusiastically. "Go on over to the house. When you get there, go to the next-door neighbors, the green house, and ask them to let you in; they have a key. Take a look around, and when you're done call me and let me know if you want to make the owner an offer. Oh, by the way, if you have any questions about the house, the neighbors can probably answer them. Okay?

I'll wait to hear back from you. Bye!"

She hangs up and waits for the phone to ring again.

❧

Jeanine is trying to sell real estate by remote control. She's sitting in her office while the sale of the house depends on what happens across town. She's relying on the neighbors to do her work for her. She has her newly printed business cards and her new suit, and she's reading about how to sell effectively, but she's not *there*.

I wonder if sometimes we take this same approach to following Christ. We have our Bibles on our bookcases and we read about how to live Christian lives, and we go to church and listen to a Christian radio station—but are we *there*, where Christianity meets the world?

Remember Grace, whose friends were concerned about her friendship with a non-Christian? Grace isn't standing on the sidelines while others bring Christ to the world. She's *there*, giving a nonChristian a closeup view of what Christian life looks like.

Deborah, the biblical prophetess who led Israel during the period of the judges, had a hands-on approach to getting things done. When her lieutenant, Barak, said he wouldn't lead the troops into battle unless she went, too, she could have simply demanded that he go. Instead, she dove in with "Very well, I'll go with you." She didn't have to, but she did. She was willing to be there.

The Lord Jesus' ministry was the same way. He circulated throughout the marketplaces, town squares, synagogues, and homes—preaching, teaching, and healing. He didn't lock Himself away and delegate others to do His work for Him. He touched crippled and deformed bodies with His own hands; He preached God's message with His own mouth and suffered the pain of crucifixion with His own body. That doesn't sound like a Savior who calls us to sit on the sidelines.

Let's look in on Jeanine again.

Her friend, Marie, is scheduled for a biopsy at the out-patient surgery clinic on Wednesday. She calls Jeanine Sunday night, in tears, and says, "I'm so scared. I can't imagine what I'll do if the news is bad. I really need moral support. Will you go with me to the clinic Wednesday?"

"Sure," Jeanine says. "When do you need me to pick you up?"

Wednesday morning, Jeanine shows up as planned. She drives Marie to the clinic, and stops the car in front of the main entrance.

"Okay," she says cheerfully, "good luck, and call me when you're done."

"Can't you come in and wait with me?" Marie asks.

"Oh, no," Jeanine says. "I don't like waiting—you know me, busy, busy, busy. And besides, hospitals make me edgy."

Jeanine seems to want to remain as removed from Marie's life as she did from the sale of the house—to conduct her friendship from a distance. She wants to stay on the sidelines while her friend is struggling through a frightening and lonely experience.

Parenting by remote control doesn't work, either. We cannot teach our children Christian values or be an example of daily Christian living from a distance. We can't delegate the task to teachers, babysitters, daycare workers, school administrators, television, movies, our parents and other family members, or even Sunday school volunteers. Parenthood is the original hands-on job!

When a child asks, "Why aren't Uncle Jay and Aunt Ruth married anymore?" do we choose the Jeanine-style approach and say "Ask them"? Or do we seize the opportunity to tell the child what God intends for marriage and why human beings sometimes can't make it work?

"I will go with you," Deborah told Barak as they headed into battle. "Surely I am with you always," the Lord Jesus told His disciples

(Matthew 28:20).

We are called to live in active service, to do God's work and live by His commands in the trenches of daily life, not on the sidelines. Doesn't that sound a lot more exciting than waiting for the phone to ring?

❧PRAYER❧

God, a passive life is easier than
the life of active involvement
that You require of Your people.
Break through my passive spirit, Lord.
Fill my heart with a yearning to be where
Christ meets the world, and let the world
meet Him through me.
AMEN.

TWENTY-THREE

TO DO, OR NOT TO DO?

*I know that nothing good lives in me,
that is, in my sinful nature.
For I have the desire to do what is good,
but I cannot carry it out.
For what I do is not the good I want to do;
no, the evil I do not want to do—
this I keep on doing.*

Romans 7:18-19

TODAY'S TO-DO LIST

- Strengthen my resistance to temptation to do what is wrong
- Practice "giving in" to impulses to do good

Your son needs a dozen plastic cups to use for a school project. There are several new boxes of them in the coffee room at work. Would you take a dozen home for him to use?

You've had the feeling your neighbor's fun-loving, good-looking husband has his eye on you. One morning, he calls you at work and invites you to have lunch with him that day. Would you go?

Your friends are all going to the mall after work, but you don't have any cash on you. One of them suggests you borrow from petty cash and pay it back the next day. Would you?

Your friend Gail has spent a whole tearful evening telling you how troubled her marriage is and how frustrated she is with her teenage son. The next day at work, someone says, "Gail isn't herself lately. Do you know what's wrong with her?" What would you say?

Temptation is all around us. Temptation to steal from our employer's time or resources. Temptation to yield to sexual attractions outside marriage. Temptation to betray a confidence.

The Bible tells us that "those who belong to Christ Jesus have crucified the sinful nature with its passions and desires" (Galatians 5:24). It's reassuring to know that sin no longer has us in its death-producing grip. However, because we're human, we still feel the pull of temptation, and we aren't always able to summon the strength from within to overcome it. We give in. Praise God that His forgiveness is always available to us! How agonizing it would be to think that our sins would cause God to abandon us.

So we keep trying, praying for power from God's Spirit to help us resist temptation and live the pure lives He desires for us. Each time we resist or overcome temptation, we grow a little stronger, a little better equipped for the next time. We grow more and more able to do what's right when we're faced with sin and temptation.

There is another kind of temptation in our lives, though. The reverse of temptation to sin is the "temptation" to do good.

Though we are tempted by our lower nature to do things we know are wrong, conversely the Holy Spirit in us prompts us to do good things. How many times have you felt moved to reach out to an ill neighbor, do something really special for your child's birthday, give money to a charity, share the workload of a stressed-out coworker? Think about people throughout history who were moved to do great, humanitarian works for humankind and great deeds for the Kingdom of God. These people gave in to temptation—the nudging of the Holy Spirit.

When we are tempted to do sinful things, God's Spirit gives us the strength to resist. In a similar way, when we are tempted, or moved, to act with kindness or love, often our lower nature steps in and tries to stop us. Satan's voice tells us, "Don't bother," "It's too hard," "It costs too much," "Look at the risks," "You're too busy." Much of the time, we decide it wasn't a good idea after all. And one less good deed is accomplished in the world.

Fighting the pressure of the lower nature can be as frustrating in this context as fighting the temptation to sin. The apostle Paul himself felt that frustration keenly: "I find this law at work: When I want to do good, evil is right there with me. For in my inner being I delight in God's law; but I see another law at work in the members of my body" (Romans 7:21-23).

Maybe Paul was thinking of this same battle when he wrote to the Galatians: "Let us not become weary in doing good, for at the proper time we will reap a harvest if we do not give up" (6:9). It's usually easier to give in to sin than to resist; by the same token, it's easier to let fatigue or fear or uncertainty conquer our good impulses before we carry them out. But since when were Christians committed to taking the easy route?

God challenges us to live lives of kindness and compassion, bearing burdens for others and ministering to the needy. If we let the lower nature defeat our loving impulses, God's work will not get done. Just as a part of Christian growth is learning to resist temptation to sin, another part is learning to give in when the Spirit prompts us to do good.

❧PRAYER❧

*Loving Father, give me the courage to do
what needs to be done. Help me not
to be swayed by worldly voices saying
that it's too difficult or too risky or too costly.
Through Your Spirit, may I be strong enough
to resist the temptation to do evil and yield
to the temptation to do good.*
AMEN.

TWENTY-FOUR

BRING ON THE CHEER-LEADING SQUAD

*May our Lord Jesus Christ himself
and God our Father, who loved us and by
his grace gave us eternal encouragement
and good hope, encourage your hearts
and strengthen you in every good
deed and word.*

2 Thessalonians 2:16

TODAY'S TO-DO LIST

☞ Practice the art of giving encouragement to others

M y mother is an amazing person. Spend an hour with her and you'll leave believing you are the most interesting, talented, capable, wonderful person in the world. She just has that effect on people. She has the gift of encouragement.

The word at the heart of encouragement is *courage*. When we encourage another person, we stoke up her spirit, build her confidence, give her courage to do what she needs to do or face what she needs to face.

Encouragement was a precious gift in the early church. Imagine these newly formed clusters of believers, fighting to establish their small communities of faith in the face of persecution, doubt, ridicule, and danger. It's no wonder that the apostle Paul and other leaders of the early church so insistently urged their brothers and sisters to "encourage one another and build each other up" (1 Thessalonians 5:11).

The early church leader Barnabas was especially noted for his gift of encouragement as well as his love and generosity. In fact, his name means "Son of Encouragement" (Acts 4:36)!

People today—both inside and outside the church—need courage, too. Maybe an encouraging word from you is what a friend or family member needs to help him or her . . .

. . . withstand the nagging of self-doubt.

. . . rise above disappointment and setbacks.

. . . maintain hope in the face of tragedy.

. . . resist giving up when the demands of life seem overwhelming.

The opposite of encouragement, of course, is *dis*couragement. Discouragement happens when something diminishes our optimism, defeats our hopes and erodes our courage. As Christians, heirs to the most glorious of hopes, we are not to be in the business of discouragement. We are to build others up, recognize them as children of God, encourage them to seek the abundant life He offers.

In so many situations of our day-to-day lives, we have the choice between giving an encouraging word and a discouraging one, between building up and tearing down. For example:

Darlene's mother has been seriously ill for several weeks. As her neighbor, you can see that Darlene is about to collapse from the strain of running back and forth to the hospital and the uncertainty of not knowing from day to day what her mother's condition will be. You could say:

> *Discouraging word:* "I know how you feel. When my father was sick like that, the strain about killed my mother and me. He stayed that way for three years, too."
>
> *Encouraging word:* "I know your mother appreciates your spending so much time at the hospital and taking care of everything at her house. I'm sure she'd understand if you took an evening off to relax and go to bed early."

Your assistant at work prepared a document for you but used the wrong format and you really need for her to do it over. You could say:

> *Discouraging word:* "This is all wrong. You'll have to do it over this way."
>
> *Encouraging word:* "I like the way this is

set up; it looks very professional. Unfortunately, the boss expects it to be in a different format. Let me show you how to do it."

Your friend Liz, who has a full-time job and two high-school age kids, confides to you that she's considering going back to school to get a degree in business. You could say:

Discouraging word: "You'd be a wreck! I don't know how you think you could juggle that plus your job and the kids. And if you only take one course a semester, it'll take you forever!"

Encouraging word: "That's great! With all the work experience you already have, you'll have a head start on those wide-eyed college freshmen!"

You're about to have company, and your six-year-old has built an intricate structure of blocks in the middle of the family room. You really want the house to look nice—for a change—when your company comes. You could say:

Discouraging word: "Get all your junk out of the family room! I'm having company! Put all the blocks back in the box, too."

Encouraging word: "Your castle is beautiful, and I know it was a lot of work. Would you please pick up all the other toys in the family room so that no one will accidentally knock it over?"

Here's a challenge for us to take on: Let's be the modern-day female counterparts of the early church's Barnabas: "Daughters of Encouragement"!

❦PRAYER❦

*Gracious God, give me the vision
to see when others are in need of encouragement. Let me give encouragement lavishly,
generously, and wholeheartedly,
always choosing the kind word over
the sharp one, to build up others
rather than tear them down.*
AMEN.

TWENTY-FIVE

HURRY UP!

*I was shown mercy so that in me,
the worst of sinners, Christ Jesus might
display his unlimited patience.*

1 Timothy 1:16

TODAY'S TO-DO LIST

⚹ Practice being more patient—with God, with myself, with my children, and with others

The freeway is gridlocked. You're running late to pick up the kids at the daycare center. Four cars ahead of you, a driver gets out and raises the hood of his car; he's stalled. *Patience!*

Patience—we need it every single day. But in our fast-food, fast-fix culture, are we in danger of forgetting how to be patient? As Christians, we can't afford to forget. According to God's Word, patience is an essential quality of the Spirit, an integral part of day-to-day Christian living.

We often think of patience in relation to waiting, when the timetable of people or events isn't the same as ours. In that sense, patience means a willingness to wait without complaining or becoming frustrated and angry. It's the type of patience we need when traffic is backed up or the dentist's office is running behind schedule.

The Bible shows us, though, that there is much more than that to the quality of patience. Its many facets can serve us well in virtually every area of life.

Jane's new coworker at the office, Kelly, is having trouble learning to use the company's computer system. She's interrupted Jane so many times in the last hour to ask for help that now she's beginning to ask questions Jane's already answered. Jane finds herself clenching her teeth every time she hears Kelly saying, "Umm, excuse me . . . again."

Patience is often coupled in Scripture with kindness. The patient person is generous-spirited toward other people, compassionate and accepting of their foibles and quirks. Demonstrating patience is not simply answering a coworker's questions over and over; it's doing so in a genuine spirit of helpfulness and support, rather than in a grudging or irritated way. Paul wrote, "We urge you, brothers . . . encourage the timid, help the weak, be patient with everyone" (1 Thessalonians 5:14).

Debra is trying to throw together a quick dinner, sandwiched in between arriving home from work and taking her daughter to soccer practice. Her husband comes home from work and says, "Remember, we planned to go over those tax papers tonight. I have to leave for a meeting in a little while, so can we do it now?" Debra catches herself just in time, preventing an angry retort about obviously having her hands full at the moment.

Another element of patience is self-control, an ability to keep ourselves from losing our restraint under pressure. "A patient man has great understanding, but a quick-tempered man displays folly," Solomon wrote (Proverbs 14:29). Whether it's an eruption of anger at a child, or a sharp retort to a spouse or coworker, patience can keep us from doing something we'd wish later we hadn't.

Gina's thirteen-year-old daughter, Stacy, is furious because Gina wouldn't let her buy the outfit she wanted for her friend's party this weekend. Gina's reasons were (1) it was outrageously expensive and (2) it made Stacy look, well, like a tramp. Now Stacy's being surly and sarcastic, yelling at her little brother and giving Gina the cold shoulder. Gina's sure she's grown five new gray hairs in the last twelve hours.

On occasion, parenting requires the exercise of all the aspects of patience we've listed: willingness to wait (until Stacy's tantrum blows over *and* until she's past adolescence); kindness and acceptance (maintaining a firm-but-loving attitude, while bearing in mind that Stacy is acting like a normal thirteen-year-old); and self-control (to keep from saying something angry and hurtful, or renting Stacy to the neighbors until she's twenty-one).

There are days when Linda still can't believe her husband has left. All the anger, all the trying again, all the lawyers' meetings are behind her now, but she never knew it would hurt so much for so long. She knows that, ultimately, time will make it hurt less, but right now she wishes she could wave a magic wand and feel like a whole person again.

Patience includes an element of endurance, an ability to withstand adversity without losing hope. "Be joyful in hope, patient in affliction, faithful in prayer," Paul encouraged the Christians in the church at Rome (Romans 12:12).

The patient person is able to endure the present because she can see beyond it. She is willing to wait on God's work in her life, knowing that His timetables are not the same as ours, but that He never fails us. King David wrote in the psalms, "I waited patiently for the LORD; he turned to me and heard my cry" (40:1).

❧PRAYER❧

Lord, teach me patience in all its aspects.
Teach me to love those who try my patience
and to treat them with true kindness.
Allow me to experience the peace that comes
from waiting patiently for You.
AMEN.

TWENTY-SIX

THE PARABLE OF THE TERRIBLE CHILD

*Train a child in the way he should go,
and when he is old
he will not turn from it.*

Proverbs 22:6

TODAY'S TO-DO LIST

☞ Reaffirm my commitment to Christian parenting

☞ Practice dealing with my children in the same model of love and discipline with which God deals with me

O nce upon a time, there was a very terrible child named Jeremy. When Jeremy was two, he screamed and whined every night because he couldn't eat candy at dinner. His mother explained that candy is a special treat, but good food is what makes our bodies strong and healthy. Jeremy didn't listen. His mom left his dinner in front of him and left the candy in the candy jar. Eventually he always ate his dinner.

When Jeremy was five, his mother, who worked in a bank, had to take time off from work to go to kindergarten and meet with his teacher.

"Jeremy needs to start learning to get along with others," the teacher said. "He takes toys away from the other children and won't give them back. He makes up stories and gets the other children to believe them. He has convinced them that if they dig a big enough hole in the playground, they can escape to China where children don't have to go to school."

"Tell me a story, Jeremy," his mom said that day on the way home from kindergarten. Jeremy told her a very clever story about a fish that lived in a little boy's bathtub and helped him with his swimming lessons.

"You're very good at making up stories, Jeremy," his mother said. "But it's important not to tell people stories just to make them believe things that aren't true. Now I'm going to tell you a story."

And she told him a story about a little boy whose friend at school took his toys away and wouldn't give them back. They talked about how that made the little boy feel.

In the third grade, Jeremy's mother had to leave work and go to school to pick Jeremy up because the school nurse called and said Jeremy was sick and asking to go home.

On the way home, his mother asked him what was wrong with him. "Nothing," Jeremy answered cheerfully. "I just didn't want to be in school today."

"You lied about being sick," his mother said. "That was wrong. And I want you to stay in your room today and think about why lying is wrong. We've talked about it before."

"You mean I can't go over to Jimmy's to play?"

"No," she said.

About an hour later he came up to her and said, "I know now why lying is wrong."

"Why?" his mom asked.

"Because it gets you in trouble," Jeremy answered.

"No, that's not why—although it does," his mother said. And then she explained to him that God wants us to tell the truth. Otherwise, people can't trust us and we can't trust them, and people have to be honest with each other to get along.

"I understand now," Jeremy said, "so can I go to Jimmy's?" When his mother said no, he said, "Then I'll just sit up here in my room and yell out the window 'My mom is the meanest mom in the world.'"

"Okay," his mom said, going out and closing the door.

Jeremy yelled for about twenty minutes and fell asleep.

When he got into middle school, Jeremy's grades were barely good enough for him to pass from one grade to the next. His mother explained that if he didn't study, he wouldn't be able to go to college and become a writer like he wanted to, but he still didn't study.

Finally, his mother took time off work and went to see his teachers. Every night after that, no matter how tired she was after working at the bank, she went through his list of assignments and made sure he had done them all.

In high school, Jeremy played football. His mother went to every game, and even stayed after Jeremy had gotten thrown out for fighting.

"That guy made me mad," Jeremy would say when his mother asked him why he was fighting.

"That doesn't make it okay," his mother said.

Jeremy graduated from high school. Because his mother had saved enough money, he was able to go to college. His mother wrote to him every week.

Eventually, Jeremy graduated from college. He had been accepted for a job with a magazine, writing funny stories. His mother, his aunt, and his uncle went to the graduation ceremony.

Afterward, Jeremy and his mom were talking. They reminisced about things Jeremy did when he was younger.

"I was a terrible child, wasn't I?" Jeremy asked his mother.

"Yes, you were," she answered. "But I loved you more than anything in the world. And I still do."

"I know," Jeremy said. "I knew it all along."

❧PRAYER❧

Dear heavenly Father,
I marvel at these children
You have entrusted to me. I need Your help
so that I'll never take lightly
the responsibility of parenthood,
and never let other tasks become
more important. And above all,
may I never, never give up.
AMEN.

PART FOUR

AND NOW, MY FAMOUS JUGGLING ACT

TWENTY-SEVEN

PRIME TIME

He has showed me, O man, what is good.
And what does the LORD require of you?
To act justly and to love mercy and
to walk humbly with your God.

Micah 6:8

S arah is just tidying up her desk, getting ready to go home at the end of a hectic workday. She's glad it's almost quitting time; she's more than ready to get away from the office.

As she's putting away the last stack of papers, she thinks about her agenda for that evening. Her daughter's piano recital starts at seven. Her best friend, Julie, has been asking her to come by to see her new baby, and Sarah thought she might do that tonight. In addition, her mother has been ill but is feeling better now, and Sarah was thinking about taking her to the mall tonight. And Sarah's exercise class, which she's missed for over two weeks, starts at 7:30.

How, Sarah asks herself, *do all these*

things manage to be competing for my time in this one evening? She wonders if it would be simpler just to stay at work!

When we find ourselves in a time bind like this, how can we make sensible, realistic choices that enable us not only to fulfill our commitments, but to feel good about the choices we've made—and not wear ourselves out with chronic over-commitment? Let's look at some practical questions we can ask to help us make these choices.

Is it a once-in-a-lifetime event? Maybe Sarah's daughter has a piano recital every month or several times a year, so the one tonight is just one of several. On the other hand, maybe this is the first-ever, or most important, or the culmination of months of work. Sarah can weigh the specific circumstances in deciding how important it is for her to be there.

Can it be rescheduled? Surely her friend Julie would understand if Sarah asked to come see the baby this weekend instead. Sometimes relieving the pressure of a jammed-up schedule is as simple as rescheduling, rather than seeing all commitments as now-or-never events.

Can two or more activities be combined? Since Sarah's goal in taking her mother to the mall was just to give her a chance to get out of the house, inviting her mother to the piano recital or to see Julie's baby could achieve the same goal while eliminating some of the time conflict.

How important is my participation to the other people involved? In our effort to be supportive to friends and loved ones, I think we often overestimate the importance of our participation in some of their activities. After years of unenthusiastically attending each other's work-related social functions, my husband and I finally have begun asking each other, "Is it important to you for me to attend this?" when an event comes up. We no longer assume that it's vitally important to the other person for us to be there.

What will the consequences be? Sometimes our best course is to examine the consequences of choosing one commitment over another. Will your job really be in jeopardy if you miss the company's annual picnic and go to your son's science fair instead, or will you just miss out on those few extra brownie points you might have earned for being at the picnic? Will your grandmother be devastated if you bring the kids over for a visit next Saturday instead of this Saturday because you promised a friend you'd help her move to her new apartment? If you cancel out on helping your friend, will she be left with no one to help her move, or are there others who can fill in for you?

What choice is most in keeping with my priorities? This, of course, is the key question. We are doomed to flounder in the quicksand of conflicting desires and commitments until we have a clear sense of priorities.

What *is* most important to you? Rearing Christian children? Creating a stable, loving home? Being a witness for Christ to those around you?

Knowing our own priorities is the best tool for simplifying the task of decision-making. It gives us guidelines for making choices, and more importantly, it gives us peace of mind, stemming from the knowledge that we have made a sound choice. Knowing our priorities saves us from constantly second-guessing our decisions or feeling guilty every time we have to choose between two or more commitments.

When our foremost desire is to please the Lord, I don't think it matters whether we choose the basketball game or the board meeting, the company picnic or the church seminar. I believe that God honors our desire to please Him. When we truly seek to make the choice most in keeping with His commands and Christ's example, we can be confident that our choices will be right in His eyes.

☙PRAYER❧

*Dear Lord God, thank You for the freedom
to choose how to invest my time, energy,
and ability. Help me to always honor
You in the choices I make.
Thank You that I can experience peace
with the choices I have made, when I make
them on the basis of Your commands
and Christ's example.*

AMEN.

TWENTY-EIGHT

WHERE'S THE NEAREST HOLE?

I love you, O LORD, my strength.
The LORD is my rock, my fortress and my
deliverer; my God is my rock, in whom I
take refuge. He is my shield and the horn
of my salvation, my stronghold.

Psalm 18:1-2

TODAY'S TO-DO LIST

✍ Learn to seek help from God and from others during the low periods of my life

We've talked about the importance of giving encouragement to others. But what about those times when *we* need building up, reassurance, and an encouraging word? You know, those times when we feel like . . .

   . . . a balloon with a slow leak,
   . . . a ball of yarn the cat has played with,
   . . . a candy bar on a hot sidewalk,
   . . . a squashed grape,
   . . . the person in a TV commercial for a pounding-headache remedy.

Even those of us who often experience the deep-down peace and joy of knowing Christ have periods when life just doesn't feel "right." We feel spiritually weak; we feel that we're failing in some important area. Maybe we're beginning to lose hope that things are ever going to be better. Or maybe we sense that we're spinning our wheels, racing madly through life but going nowhere. Or maybe we feel *Blah* with a capital B.

There are no easy formulas or fast fixes that can banish these low periods from our lives, but God's Word does promise that He desires for us to be restored to joy and wholeness.

What steps can we take to put ourselves on the road to this restoration?

Pray. As in all times of our lives, we need to pray. Not just once, like slapping a bandage on a cut, but regularly, consistently, and frequently. As in many things, we reap the benefits of prayer largely in proportion to what we put into it. So praying "Lord, fix my life" probably won't benefit us as much as more thoughtful prayer. How can we pray "thoughtfully"?

First, we begin by praising God for His goodness and thanking Him for His blessings. This helps us focus on who He is and on the good things He has given us, rather than starting our prayer with a poor-me attitude.

Second, we ask God to give us specific spiritual blessings to deal with the current situation: wisdom and insight to see solutions (or maybe to know what the problem is!); discernment to distinguish right choices from wrong ones; compassion in dealing with people problems; patience to avoid making rash decisions or acting on emotional impulses; courage to take risks or face the consequences of difficult choices. The important thing is to identify exactly what it is that we desire from God.

Third, we ask Him for His guidance in the days ahead, as we seek to make changes that will bring restoration and healing in our lives. We ask for His guidance in making right choices, in recognizing people and events that can help us, and in applying His commands on a day-to-day basis.

Fourth, we again thank Him—this time for the assurance that He hears us, that we are never alone, and that He is always faithful.

Enlist help. Go to people you trust and who you feel have something helpful to offer you. Ask them specific questions to elicit the information you need: How do you juggle your job and the kids without being burnt out all the time? How do you and your husband manage to maintain and grow in your relationship? What do you do when your job and family commitments come into conflict? How do you handle it when your supervisor constantly expects too much of you?

Of course, it's important to choose these people carefully and reflect on their advice before acting on it. Be sure it's compatible with your Christian values and practical in your specific situation. Even if you can't use their suggestions, their experiences may give you new ideas or new ways of looking at things.

Give. One unfortunate byproduct of down times in our lives is self-centeredness. We begin to be so absorbed in our problems that we lose sight of the needs of others. Making a gesture of generosity or kindness reminds us that there are needs in the world besides our own and helps us keep our perspective. Giving also acts as a tonic for the weary spirit.

Find a worthwhile volunteer project and pitch in. Drive an elderly person to church or make a friendly phone call to someone who wouldn't expect it. Make a small gift for a friend just to say, "Thanks for being you."

God wants us to live rich, satisfying, abundant lives. When we find we're not doing that, it's up to us to seek His help. When we commit ourselves fully to a healing partnership with Him, we've taken the first step in climbing out of the valley and onto the peak.

❧PRAYER❧

*Lord, sometimes my life feels like
it's "out of order." Don't let me wallow
in self-pity or anger because things
aren't the way I want them to be.
Give me the wisdom to seek You
and the courage to make changes.*
AMEN.

TWENTY-NINE

WELL, LORD, THERE WAS THIS BANANA

*"They have . . . ears to hear
but do not hear,
for they are a rebellious people."*
Ezekiel 12:2

"Consider carefully what you hear."
Mark 4:24

TODAY'S TO-DO LIST

⚘ Listen for God's voice amid the
  clamor of my daily life
⚘ Learn to distinguish His voice from
  mine and others

Consider this familiar motherhood experience.

You're at the church nursery, where a dozen toddlers are playing in the huge room. Suddenly one child starts to cry. You listen for all of two seconds before you know it's yours. You'd know that cry anywhere. It doesn't matter how noisy the room is or how many other children are talking, crying, playing—you know which one is yours.

We may act so distracted at work that our frustrated coworkers ask, "Are you deaf?" but when it comes to our children, our hearing is excellent. For most of us, though, it's far easier to achieve this perfect hearing in regard to our children's voices than God's. Why is that?

My friend Cathy says she wishes she had

better hearing when it comes to distinguishing God's voice from her own—the inner voice that comes from her own will and desires. We're good at convincing ourselves that what we want to do is what God wants for us, too, and sometimes it is—but not always. Yet our own voices can be very persuasive and/or very loud when we're faced with choices to make.

The voices of other people in our lives can make God's voice harder to hear, too. Others' expectations of us exert powerful forces on our decision-making. Our bosses, coworkers, children, spouses, parents, friends, fellow church members, business acquaintances, and others all have their ideas of who we should be and what we should be doing.

Because human beings are the way they are, these individuals' agendas for us are often—although certainly not always—an unpredictable mixture of self-interest and genuine concern. Their voices may challenge us to seek what is truly best, or they may demand that we conform to *their* ideas about what is best. Or, in their efforts to be supportive, they may try to say what they think we want to hear rather than what we *need* to hear.

Our society has a loud, raucous, insistent voice of its own, which comes to us primarily through the media. It tells us to do what feels good . . . to strive for a lifestyle that enables us to have and do whatever we want . . . to make sure no one gets ahead of us in the race for success . . . to resist any restrictions on our freedom of self-indulgence.

God's voice has so much competition. How can we filter through all the noise so that we can better hear His words of encouragement and guidance?

First, we need to be *attuned* enough to distinguish His voice from others that might only appear to be from Him. Satan loves to masquerade as God in any way he can. He loves to deceive. He uses the world's attractions to appeal to our egos and our selfish desires. He encourages us to focus on what *we* want and then try to make God fit into our plans, rather than focusing on what God wants for us.

He may use other people, even Christians, to deceive us. They, like us, are subject to human error. Their advice, as well as our own counsel, needs to be scrutinized against the standards of God's Word.

Paul told the Christians in Philippi, "This is my prayer: that your love may abound more and more in knowledge and depth of insight, so that you may be able to discern what is best" (1:9-10).

Second, we need to be *alert* so that we

don't simply miss what God wants us to hear. Our alertness falters when we become totally focused on what is happening around us, totally caught up in the frustrations, temptations, and concerns of daily living.

Remember this old-time comedy routine?

"Excuse me, sir, you have a banana in your ear."

"Pardon?"

"I said, you have a banana in your ear."

"Sorry, I can't hear you. I have a banana in my ear."

Our lives are full of bananas—split-second schedules, kids with colds, work conflicts, overtime, stress, fatigue, you name it. It's hard to hear God's voice amid the trials of daily life that demand our attention.

Yes, we have to deal with these things, but we also need to keep our heavenly perspective. We can do it by reserving a quiet place in our hearts and minds, amid the chaos, where we cherish and store up the things of God and meditate on what they mean in our lives. If we lose this quiet place, we hinder our ability to hear His voice.

In the next chapter, we'll look more closely at how God speaks to us and how we can distinguish His voice from the others that clamor for our attention.

May all our bananas be in fruit salads.

❧PRAYER❧

Dear Lord, grant me discernment,
to know what is right and to be able
to see what is from You, versus what
is from the world. Clear that all-important
space in my heart where I go
to listen for You. I want to hear
Your voice when You speak.
AMEN.

THIRTY

DO YOU HEAR WHAT I HEAR?

Now choose life so that you and your children may live and that you may love the LORD your God, listen to his voice, and hold fast to him. For the LORD is your life.

Deuteronomy 30:19-20

TODAY'S TO-DO LIST

✎ Become more alert to ways God speaks to me
✎ Make a greater effort to hear God's voice daily

J anet has been offered a new job. The salary is better than what she's currently making. The job is at a higher level than her current one and involves some travel, which appeals to her.

She feels some vague reservations about it, though. And she sincerely wants to do what's right in God's sight. She prays about it. She talks to her husband, her children, her parents, her friends, even her minister. She hears a dozen voices in her head, all clamoring to cast the deciding vote.

Her husband's voice: "Well, the extra money would be nice, and I know you like a new challenge. But the traveling worries me— I can't see how we would work out the logistics. And you're already so stressed out; do you really want a job that's *more* demanding?"

Her friend Jeannette, who works in her current office: "If I were you, I'd take any chance to get out of here! You know that there's no way for you to move up in this company in even the remotely foreseeable future. Your talents are going to waste here. Go for it!"

Her mother: "Do what will make you happiest, dear."

Her friend Susan, who's in her Bible study: "I don't know, Janet. Can Jeff handle the household by himself if you're traveling? Even when you're in town, you'll have night meetings and late hours like you do now. Won't you miss a lot with the kids?"

Her own voice: "I've worked so hard for an opportunity like this. Maybe with the extra money we could make that trip to Hawaii we've always talked about. I'd have a private office, a position on the senior management staff, many people reporting to me—big-time stuff! Of course, it'll be hard on Jeff and the kids, but we can work it out. We always have . . . I guess."

I believe each of us, as working mothers, can identify with Janet's dilemma. Like us, she has so many important considerations to sort out and prioritize: her family's well-being; effective use of her own time, energy, and talent; looking to the future; financial needs and desires; pressure to conform to the world's values—it's a tough decision! How can she hear God's voice above the clamor?

God deals with every one of His children differently, and each of us hears His voice uniquely when we're faced with a decision. However, from my own experience and what others have shared with me, His voice in our hearts usually seems to have one or more of the following characteristics.

God's voice often comes unexpectedly. An uneasiness, a hopefulness, a totally new perspective, a sudden sense of peace, a nagging question—His voice may take many forms, but it often seems to come out of the blue, not necessarily when we're concentrating on the decision itself.

It comes from more than one source. A line from a hymn you sing in church on Sunday sticks in your brain. A friend makes an observation that seems to cut right to the heart of the question. Your Bible reading for the day yields a flash of insight. And all these things point in the same direction.

God's voice is persistent. Your strong sense that course A or course B is the right one seems to stay with you as other options fade away. It may not be the option favored by others; in fact, they may all tell you you're crazy, but your sense of its rightness persists.

It is consistent with God's Word and His commands. God does not contradict Himself. If we're leaning toward a decision for reasons that are contrary to Scripture—a choice motivated solely by financial gain to meet our own desires, for example—then we are not being guided by God's voice.

God's voice is consistent with traditional Christian values. The importance of the family, the sanctity of marriage, the mandate to serve God through acts of charity and service, the instruction to set time aside for worship and fellowship—these values must be respected as we make our decisions. Choices that violate these values—subordinating our role as wives or mothers, for example, or disrupting our time for worship—are not God-directed.

It does not conform to the world's values. If Janet chose to base her decision solely on the world's standards, she wouldn't even have a decision to make—she'd take the new job. It offers all the things the world wants: status, power, money, the trappings of success. However, voices that tell us to choose the new job based on these values are not from God.

God does speak to us. We may hear Him loud and clear, or we may have to say,

"Pardon?" or, "Could You please speak up?" We may need to exercise a great deal of patience, maybe more than we thought we had.

But if we listen with a believing heart, we will indeed hear Him.

❧PRAYER❧

Dear gracious God,
it amazes me that in Your infinite greatness,
You still talk to me in the personal,
individual, unique way of a loving Father.
I marvel that, overcoming my tiny,
limited understanding, You find ways
to make Your voice heard in my heart.
I praise You because Your glory is
too great to comprehend.
AMEN.

THIRTY-ONE

I'M JUST LETTING OFF STEAM

*Make every effort to add to your faith
goodness; and to goodness, knowledge;
and to knowledge, self-control;
and to self-control, perseverance;
and to perseverance, godliness.*

2 Peter 1:5-6

TODAY'S TO-DO LIST

❧ Find constructive ways to "let off steam" when pressure in my life builds up

Today's fast-paced, schedule-driven, frantically busy lifestyle is often described as "life in a pressure cooker." Although I don't own one myself, I can remember seeing and hearing the pressure cooker at work when my mother was preparing dinner. The steam valve would flip rapidly from side to side, driven by spurts of steam from inside. That steam wasn't seeping out slowly, either; it was pushing its way out forcefully, as though it *had* to escape.

We need to let off steam, too. Our lives really are much like being in a pressure cooker. Unfortunately, what often happens is that we wait until the pressure becomes intolerable, then we explode.

It's 10:00 at night and you're starting to

think you might get a chance to go to bed. Your son walks in with a dirty baseball uniform that he just remembered he needs washed for tomorrow's game.

You lose it. You scold him for waiting until the last minute and angrily point out how many other things you have to do. You express your frustration with other family members not sharing the household responsibilities. The whole time, you know it's not about the baseball uniform, and it's not about the washing—it's just the last straw.

How can we keep from letting the pressure build up to this point? By being alert to when our personal pressure level is rising, we can take some steps to relieve the pressure before it blasts out on its own. Here are some possibilities to consider.

Exercise. Yes, it sounds trite, because everyone today is praising the joys of exercise—but exercise does both physiologically and psychologically help relieve stress and tension that pressure causes.

There are all kinds of exercise options; you can join an exercise class or rent an exercise video and try it out. (Have your kids follow it with you for some extra time together.) Find some magazine articles describing various exercises and pick out the ones you like best.

Jump rope. Go swimming or jogging. Do

situps. Try a variety of exercises so you don't get bored. One warning: Don't let yourself get compulsive about exercise; you don't need one more source of pressure in your life! Do it for fun and good health; if you're not enjoying it, try something else. Recruit a friend for moral support.

Laughter is another good pressure-breaker. Poll your friends to find out what's the funniest movie they've ever seen, and rent it. Go to the library and check out a book of really, really dumb jokes. Go through back issues of *Reader's Digest* and read all the humor columns.

Find a TV sitcom that strikes your funny-bone and watch it with the family. (Be sure it's suitable for the kids.) When something funny happens during your workday, remember to share it with the family that night so you can all have a laugh. Learn to laugh out loud; you'll get a kick out of hearing yourself!

A *change of scenery* is a good way to relieve the feeling of pressure that comes from a constantly demanding routine. Being reminded that there's a world out there breaks you out of the rut of routine and the pressures that go with it.

Drive to the next town and have lunch someplace you haven't been, or take the kids to a park you haven't visited before. Shop for back-to-school clothes at a different store or mall. Read the travel section of the newspaper or a magazine article about another part of the country. If you can afford it, take a day or a weekend for a real getaway, even if it's just down the road.

Finally, think about *giving yourself a special treat*, acknowledging that you are worthy of kindness and tender loving care just as those around you are. The treat might be a luxurious bubble bath, with strict orders to the family that both you and the bathroom are off limits until you come out.

You could visit the local consignment or thrift shop and bring home a bargain blouse to make a new outfit out of an old skirt and jacket. Or treat yourself to a long-distance phone call to a friend or relative who can always be counted on for a sympathetic ear and an encouraging word.

And here's a really special treat to consider: *Give yourself the gift of an hour to do as you please—no guilty thoughts of what you* should *be doing will be allowed!*

If we live in a state of chronic pressure, these letting-off-steam strategies will help, but they'll only treat the symptoms, not cure the problem. In the next chapter we'll look at some ways to turn down the heat under the pressure cooker.

❦PRAYER❦

*Father God, I don't want to let the pressure
of daily living cheat me out of the joy
You've promised. Show me constructive ways
to let off steam and to restore
enjoyment to my life.*
AMEN.

THIRTY-TWO

I'M MAKING A FEW CUTBACKS OF MY OWN

Hear my prayer, O Lord;
listen to my cry for mercy.
In the day of my trouble I will call to you,
for you will answer me.

Psalm 86:6-7

TODAY'S TO-DO LIST

⌖ Make changes in my life to relieve
 the chronic pressure of over-
 commitment

S haron has been looking forward to
attending her daughter's school play, but
once she gets there, she can't seem to
keep her mind on the show. She and her boss
had a major disagreement that afternoon
about how the work of taking inventory
should be distributed.

*If I have to work any more overtime this
month, I'll drop from exhaustion*, she says to
herself. *The whole inventory system is so
messed up anyway; if anyone would listen to
my suggestions. . . .*

When she finally sees her daughter come
out on the stage, she has no idea what's happened in the play so far. She decides she'd
better pay more attention, but her mind
keeps drifting. She remembers she promised

the pastor she'd call some elderly members of the church. *When will I get it done?* she wonders.

Maybe I need to think about a new job, she tells herself. *But adjusting to a job change is so stressful; I don't think I'm up to it right now. Of course, I'm not sure I'm up to staying in the one I have, either. . . .*

En route home from the school, Sharon's daughter chatters excitedly. "Mom! Did you see what happened when I first came on the stage?" her daughter asks. "I was so embarrassed! Was everyone looking at me?"

Sharon's stuck. She realizes she was too preoccupied to notice what happened. She doesn't know what to say.

Sharon's life is so pressure-filled that she can't even free her mind long enough to enjoy her child's performance. She wants to be supportive and interested, but she's finding it virtually impossible to concentrate. The byproducts of pressure are destroying her enjoyment of life and her ability to be the kind of mother she wants to be.

We all have pressure in our lives, at some times more than at others. We deal with it and survive. However, pressure becomes unhealthy when we feel as though there is always something pushing us, so that we can never relax, never take time out. Our minds seem to be racing ninety miles an hour; we're preoccupied and harried. We want to slow down, but we feel like we can't.

Does this describe you? Is the pressure in your life at that level? Time for some changes!

First of all, ask yourself whether the pressure you feel is due to some temporary circumstance: you're in the middle of a super-busy season at work; the kids' school functions all seem to be scheduled for this month; your spouse is taking night classes and can't help around the house. If the current squeeze *is* temporary, let some of the household tasks or volunteer duties go for a while, or recruit family members to pitch in with a little extra help.

If, on the other hand, the situation isn't temporary, then you may need to make longer-term changes. Is your job simply too demanding to accommodate the other commitments in your life? If it is, maybe you need to set a goal of making a job change.

Are you carrying a disproportionate share of the responsibility around the house? Assign family members more active roles in household operations.

Does the word *no* get stuck in your throat when someone asks you to do something? Give yourself permission to turn down a church committee assignment or other volunteer task from time to time. Christians do have a responsibility to help meet needs, but the Bible doesn't say we have to do it all right now. "Can't" isn't a four-letter word.

Be brutal in examining your own schedule. Are you wasting time by being too particular about certain things, like cleaning the bathroom floor with a toothbrush? Use a sponge mop and there will be leftover time for something else! When your daughter goes to gymnastics class, do you feel honor-bound to sit and watch every single minute, or can you take care of a few errands while she's occupied?

When you have to wait unexpectedly at the doctor's office or for a business appointment, do you drum your fingers and listen to your blood pressure rise? How about relaxing with a magazine or book instead, or writing an overdue letter?

Finally, we need to accept that we cannot do everything. I know, I know—for superwomen like you and me, that's a hard admission. But we are not doing our loved ones or ourselves any favors by living in a state of constant fatigue and borderline explosion. We cheat them out of our full attention, our energy, and our joy, and we cheat ourselves, too.

Letting off steam isn't enough. Let's turn down the heat under the pressure cooker.

❧PRAYER❧

*Lord, I know You don't want me
to live in a constant state of overwhelming
pressure. Show me how to rest in You.
I need Your help to find peace
in the assurance that I don't have to be
all things to all people; I only have to be
the person You want me to be.*

AMEN.

THIRTY-THREE

WHAT DO YOU THINK?

*Mary treasured up all these things
and pondered them in her heart.*

Luke 2:19

TODAY'S TO-DO LIST

〰 Find time for thoughtful reflection
amid the hectic pace of my life

My father, living in a household with a wife and two daughters, was often an island of calm in a sea of frenzy. Example: It's 6:00 a.m. on the first day of our vacation. We're getting ready to load the car for the drive to our chosen vacation spot. My sister and I are frantically stuffing last-minute items in our suitcases. At last, after much exertion, the suitcases have been closed and we're ready to rush out the door.

"Okay," my dad would say, "it's time to think. Is there anything that you've forgotten to pack?" Before any trip, he always insisted that we take a moment mentally to review our packing process and be sure we'd included everything. Invariably, one or both of us would run back to our rooms for some crucial item that hadn't made it into the suitcase.

In our impatience to leave, we always had to be firmly instructed to take those few quiet moments to mentally recheck our packing. But it always paid off, sparing us the inconvenience or disappointment of doing without a favorite toy or well-worn pajamas during our vacation.

The discipline of taking time out for reflection is a hard one to develop. Just as the lure of leaving on vacation made my sister and me impatient, now it's the call of undone laundry and the pressure to be-there-on-time that keeps us from finding the quiet moments we need. In fact, I think that for most of us, having time simply to reflect on our lives and ponder ideas is so alien that we might have forgotten how to use it.

If someone handed you a half-hour of quiet time right now, how would you use it? If you're like me and most other women I know, you'd probably spend the first half of it thinking about all the other things you should be doing and the last half thinking up even more things to do!

Supposing, though, that somehow we could discipline our schedules and ourselves so that we had a small block of time, just occasionally, reserved for thoughtful reflection—not a time to organize our day, not to make phone calls, not even for Bible study, not for any kind of *doing*.

What uses could we find for that time? Here are some possibilities.

Time to savor. To reexperience a child's moment of insight or spontaneous laughter . . . to play back in your mind a boss's praise or encouragement . . . to hear again a spouse's expression of love . . . to relish the satisfaction of a job well done. If we fail to capture and savor these treasures, we lose the joy they can bring us.

Time to examine. Am I making the best use of my time with the kids? Are they each getting my full attention often enough?

How did yesterday's misunderstanding at work occur?

How sensitive am I being to my spouse's needs at this time in his life?

Am I in a rut? Why do I feel this way?

Time to check up. How am I doing at teaching the children the values they need to know for life? Am I following through when I discipline them?

Have I stuck to my commitment to Bible study and prayer time?

Am I progressing in my job, or do I feel stagnant?

Do the people I work with see Christ's

qualities in me?

Time to explore. The kids are older now . . . maybe I should look into going back to school.

What if I decided to make a major career change?

Mom and Dad have been wanting a family reunion for so many years; could I start planning one?

Sue was telling me about that exercise class she joined; maybe I'll ask her a little more about it.

All I seem to think about is my job or the family. I'd like to take a class to learn a new hobby.

Time to resolve. I'm going to be more firm with the kids about limiting television viewing.

Joe and I need an evening out together, just the two of us. I'm going to plan it.

I get so angry with myself when I get sucked into office gossip. I'm going to make it a priority to practice better self-control.

I'm going to share my testimony with each of my children individually (even though I've already done so), and seek some insight into their spiritual development.

How many more ways of using your "thinking time" could you add to this list?

So much happens to us in the course of a

day, a week, a month, a year of our lives. In order to make sense of it, we need to step back from the treadmill and reflect . . . to "treasure up all these things and ponder them" in our hearts. How about challenging yourself today to carve out some time in the next week to savor, to examine, to check up, to explore, to resolve—and who knows what else?

❦PRAYER❦

Dear God, guide me as I take time to reflect on the life You have given me. Show me how best to live for You, how to attain the joy, the peace, and the power You promise.
AMEN.

THIRTY-FOUR

HOW BIG IS BIG ENOUGH?

Now to him who is able to do immeasurably more than all we ask or imagine, according to his power that is at work within us, to him be glory in the church and in Christ Jesus throughout all generations, for ever and ever!

Ephesians 3:20-21

❧ Learn to rest in the assurance that God is big enough for any need I have

I saw a cartoon once that showed what the world looks like to a toddler. Chairs and tables were as big as skyscrapers; the family cat was the size of a bear; and all the adults in the picture were shown only from the knees down! The cartoon gave an interesting glimpse of what it's like when you're very, very small and everything and everyone around you is bigger.

Do you sometimes feel very, very small—as though everything in your life is too big for you to manage: your job, your schedule, your household, parenting, decision-making, coping, living? The very structure of our lives as working mothers, with its built-in time constraints, makes us especially vulnerable to feeling too small to deal with the sheer magnitude of our responsibilities.

We react to this feeling of inadequacy in different ways. We may feel overcome by fatigue and apathy, barely dragging ourselves through each day. We may become like hyperactive children, rushing frantically from one thing to the next. We may become workaholics, devoting all our time to our jobs and neglecting the other areas of our lives because we feel that we can't "do it all." Whatever our reaction, it stems from a sense that somehow our lives have become unmanageable and out of control.

God's design for us is just the opposite; His plan from the very beginning of creation was for men and women to "rule over . . . all the earth" (Genesis 1:26). "You made him ruler over the works of your hands; you put everything under his feet" (Psalm 8:6).

However, we cannot effectively "rule over" our own lives, much less the whole world, without God's help. Our weaknesses and limitations are just too great, and our knowledge and understanding too narrow. We are, in fact, too small.

But God is not. He can sift through the clutter of our hectic lives and bring order out of the chaos. Our role is to lean on Him. The more we relinquish control of our lives to Him, the more we regain a sense of control in our day-to-day living. We grow equal to the task before us.

My friend Katherine is a working mother whose bright, lively three-year-old, Ben, has been plagued since birth with serious health problems. Katherine began some time ago keeping a journal of her experiences and feelings, hoping it might eventually be used to encourage other parents going through similar trials. Her journal documents the emotional roller coaster she has ridden as Ben's condition has fluctuated from promising to precarious.

At one point recently, it appeared that Ben might be dependent on a kidney dialysis machine for the rest of his life. Katherine felt that this prospect was more than she could handle.

"I decided to let it all out. I started writing, and I let all my frustration and anger pour out onto the page. Through my writing, I asked God 'Why me?' over and over again. I told Him it wasn't fair; I told Him the uncertainty and worry and financial strain were wearing me and my husband out. I told Him I felt empty and inadequate to deal with the future.

"And do you know what happened? The more I wrote, the more I felt a sense of peace. The more despair I poured out, the more He filled me with assurance. By the time I finished writing, I felt renewed. All my anger and frustration were gone. I felt . . . confident. I knew for certain that everything will be all right, that God is in charge. And whatever happens, He will help us through it."

Katherine learned firsthand that God is big enough not only for our petty day-to-day concerns, but for the heaviest burdens we bear. He is even big enough to absorb our anger, our pain, and our frustration and answer them with grace, reassurance, and hope.

If He can do that, surely He can guide us through the muddy, rock-strewn waters of daily living. He can help us unclutter a crowded calendar by clarifying our priorities. He can free us from self-imposed guilt with His reassurance of forgiveness and understanding. He can replenish our limited supplies of patience, kindness, compassion, and love from His inexhaustible stores. He can restore our belief that we are important and worthwhile by His gentle voice of encouragement.

God is big enough to manage our lives, from the most critical, life-changing decision to the smallest details. Not only is He big enough, but He is also loving enough. He wants to be a part of everything we do.

Yet God's even bigger than that. The Bible tells us He is "able to do immeasurably more than all we ask or imagine" (Ephesians 3:20). When we live in constant, faithful partnership with Him we become, like Him, bigger than life.

❧PRAYER❧

Dear Father God,
when my life is out of control,
I feel so small and so alone.
Rein me back in, Lord. Let me feel
the reassurance of Your greatness,
the promise that nothing is too big—
or too small—for You to manage.
AMEN.